STAND OUT!

Branding Strategies
for
Business Professionals

Simon Vetter
with
Michael Buchanan and Karen Friend

July Publishing
Carlsbad, California

July Publishing
PO Box 629
Carlsbad, CA 92018
www.julypublishing.com

First edition, first printing

Printed in the United States of America

ISBN 0-9704379-3-5

To order this book, visit www.simonvetter.com.

STAND OUT!

This book is dedicated to my parents.

Contents

Acknowledgments ix

Once Upon a Time in Switzerland xi

How This Book Was "Born" ... And What You Can Expect from It.. xvii

Part One   A New World of Talents and Brands

Chapter 1   The New Business Landscape 21

Chapter 2   Personal Branding Philosophy 33

Part Two   Profiles of Personal Brands

Chapter 3   Nido Qubein   Being Focused 39

Chapter 4   Tony Alessandra   Finding Your Voice 57

Chapter 5   Beverly Kaye   Discovering Your Niche 69

Chapter 6   Marshall Goldsmith Becoming Well Known 79

Chapter 7   David Allen   Increasing Personal Productivity ... 93

Chapter 8   Gayle Carson   Making Things Happen 109

Chapter 9   Brian Tracy   Pushing to the Front 125

Chapter 10 Jim Kouzes   Becoming a Leader 141

Part Three   Personal Branding from Within

Chapter 11 Three Building Blocks of Personal Brand Management 161

Top Ten Rules of Personal Brand Management 185

Suggested Reading 187

References 191

About the Author 195

Acknowledgements

Any major undertaking requires the time and energy of many people. This book is no exception. A loving THANK YOU goes to:

My mom and dad, for always loving me and supporting my ventures;

Marshall Goldsmith, for his mentorship and inspiration to interview people and write their profiles;

Tony Alessandra, David Allen, Gayle Carson, Marshall Goldsmith, Beverly Kaye, Jim Kouzes, Brian Tracy and Nido Qubein, for graciously contributing their time, ideas and generous collaboration;

Adrian Huber, for stimulating me to write about this topic;

Karen Friend, for helping put my ideas on paper;

Michael Buchanan, for bringing life to this book;

Andrew Chapman, for getting the book published;

Adriane Smith, for fine-tuning and proofreading the manuscript;

My business partners, who always stood by my side; special thanks to David Glendenning;

All of my colleagues at Alliance for Strategic Leadership, whose knowledge and camaraderie will always be appreciated;

My colleagues at the Palomar Airport Toastmasters group, for their continuous encouragement and applause;

My dear friends, for their feedback, suggestions and time spent listening to me; in particular Anne Spillane, Bella Heule, Bruce Ellis, Fredi Hanser, Thomas Lehmann and Karin Steadman;

And YOU, the reader of STAND OUT!

Once Upon a Time in Switzerland...

I am a normal guy from Switzerland, born in Lucerne, and for the first 25 years I lived a pretty ordinary life. In 1992, after five years studying business and marketing at the University of Berne and working at a variety of part-time occupations, I spiced up my career with a six-month job in Greece. I worked as a mountain bike tour guide on the island of Crete during a summer season, leading daily tours across mountains, over hills, through canyons and groves of olive trees, and along the coast of that beautiful Mediterranean island. To experience a different country and culture triggered my desire to explore other parts of the world.

When I was 29 years old, I quit my well-paid and enjoyable marketing position with a Swiss seminar and conference organization in Zurich. I was ready to move on and search for a new business venture. I booked a flight to San Diego and signed up for a three-month English program in La Jolla. Prior to that, the only time I had been to the United States was a whirlwind, two-day trip to New York, so I didn't know what to expect in California.

March 16, 1997, was a turning point in my life and a day that is still vivid in my memory. It was late afternoon when I landed at San Diego's Lindbergh Field airport. I picked up my luggage – two suitcases and my mountain bike – and I stepped outside of the airport terminal. While the sun was setting on the horizon, coloring the western sky from orange to dark blue, I felt a refreshing ocean breeze on my face. I felt like I was on vacation and I said to myself, "This is a nice place to be."

By mid-June, I had finished my English studies and decided to stay in San Diego. I liked the city, lifestyle and weather so much that I wanted to live and work here. I decided to take my enthusiasm into the marketplace and find a job. I started to look for work the way I used to do it in Switzerland: browse the employment sections of local newspapers and magazines, apply for interesting jobs, and wait to hear from a company. Guess what? I didn't hear from anyone. Out of 10 applications I sent out, only one company called to confirm they received my resume. I quickly learned that there must be a better way to find work. I explained my frustration to an executive recruiter, who told me that 90 percent of jobs are never advertised. Many positions are filled through relationships and networking, so I started to develop relationships and build my own network. On a sunny summer day, I attended a lunch meeting of the local chapter of the American Society for Training & Development (ASTD) at the Handlery Hotel in Mission Valley. I entered a room with over a hundred people – mostly consultants, trainers or human resource professionals. Everyone talked to each other, and it seemed to me that they all knew each other. I stepped to the side and waited for people to approach me. After 10 minutes, I was still waiting. I thought, "Well, Simon, if you want to find a job, you need to talk to people." Approaching strangers was very uncomfortable for me, but feeling the pressure to find work, I took a deep breath and started introducing myself to people. It turned out that people were extremely welcoming, often picking up on my accent and asking me where I was from. I began to realize that these people weren't strangers at all ... just kind people who showed a genuine interest in me.

I committed to mastering the art of networking. I made a conscious effort to meet people, engage them in intelligent conversations, build rapport, show interest, leave a lasting impression, offer support and stay connected. I continued to attend a variety of events – business association talks, special interest group meetings, social gatherings and parties. One of the many people I got to know was Jan Zaragoza, a trainer and performance improvement specialist, who I met at an ASTD meeting in August 1997. She was exceptionally helpful and referred me to three people in the training industry. One of those contacts led to a job and kicked off my career in the

U.S. In October of that year, I started working in sales for an international training organization. The networking efforts had paid off!

I had never worked in sales before, so I was jumping into a new experience. My manager at the San Diego branch assigned me to the North County sales territory. With my burgundy 1987 Ford Escort – which I bought during my second week in California – I drove into a business park and went from door to door, leaving promotional material at various businesses. Within three days, I followed up with a phone call. I developed my sales skills by talking to people one-on-one, in the streets and on the phone. In particular, I learned to deal with rejection. Prospecting for clients comes along with many "no's." After a while, I learned to not take those "no's" personally and to keep my enthusiasm up. I also realized very quickly that "cold prospecting" was not the most effective use of my time. Again, I turned to networking, getting involved in professional associations (I became a board member for ASTD in 1999) and developing a referral system. With lots of dedication and long hours, I became an award winner and top sales producer during my second year with the company. As a reward, I was invited to the company's international convention in Seattle, Washington, in December 1999. I discovered that "sales" is not only an essential business function; it's also a highly reputable profession. I am thankful to have had the opportunity to learn and practice the fine art of sales for four years.

My employer eventually offered me an opportunity to participate in a variety of training programs. I attended courses in communication, presentation, interpersonal skills, leadership, management and sales, and absorbed as much as I could in order to increase my skills in those areas. I became a better listener, a more natural speaker, a better planner and time-manager, a more skilled and confident salesperson, and a more patient and balanced person in general (I continue to work on these skills as I write this ... I still have a long way to go).

The more training I received, the more my interest in teaching rose. In my first year of employment, I became an assistant instructor and two years later, a certified instructor. I discovered how much I enjoyed teaching, whether it was facilitating a course in high-impact presentation to managers or teaching public speaking to 35 business people. I discovered teaching was my passion. I had found my "calling" – or as Aristotle put it, the place "where your talents and the needs of the world cross."

It took me more than 30 years to uncover my calling. I love to teach. It's exciting, rewarding and fulfilling to work with people, provide knowledge, increase their awareness, change behavior or help them gain new skills. It gets me up in the morning. I like teaching in a variety of different settings, such as one-on-one coaching, facilitating a workshop, presenting to a management team, teaching a teleclass, speaking in public or writing this book. In my current work, I mix the different forms according to the needs of the clients. I am now part of an international business alliance, called the Alliance for Strategic Leadership (A4SL). We are a group of over 60 "teachers" – consultants, trainers, coaches and speakers – who provide a stream of services to organizations – small to large, local to global – in the areas of leadership development, organizational change, strategy implementation and management philosophy.

The corresponding side to teaching is learning. I am a lifelong student, and I continue to learn, grow my mind, expand my horizon, take on new habits and explore new topics (such as cultures, countries and continents). The more I learn, the more I recognize how much more I can learn. It's like climbing up a mountain. The higher you go, the further you see; the more opportunities you conceive, the more interesting the world becomes. I believe that in a fast moving, technology-driven, highly competitive world, learning provides a competitive advantage for organizations as well as individuals. I am convinced that learning is a necessity for survival. In other words, if we continuously learn, we grow and we progress. If we don't learn, we stagnate and then regress.

My deep conviction about the rising demand for learning and my zeal for teaching is a major reason for writing this book. On one hand, I get to learn about personal brand management from renowned business educators, recognized thought leaders and authorities in consulting, coaching, professional speaking and training. On the other hand, this book provides a medium to teach important subject matter on a topic that I am fascinated about and that, more than ever, has become increasingly relevant in the modern business world where job security and employer loyalty is declining.

From observing the workplace, talking to all kinds of business professionals, reading current business magazines and books, and working with different companies around the world, I have noticed that more and more business people have an increasing need in four areas:

- **A strong desire for meaningful work:** Being content with work (how many people do you know who can say that?); work that is in alignment with their own values; work as self- actualization or life expression; the feeling of making a difference; contributing to a good cause.

- **A craving for recognition and belonging:** Feeling like part of a team; being understood; getting noticed for their performance; receiving recognition or appreciation; contributing ideas and being heard; getting promoted.

- **A desire for more independence:** More self-determination; having flexible work hours; taking more vacation; spending more quality time with family; working from home and avoiding those two-hour commutes.

- **An aspiration to make more money:** Increasing salary; establishing financial security; paying the mortgage without worries; being fairly compensated for their services; supporting a lifestyle; providing for their family.

If you recognize these needs within yourself, this book is for you. It will give you new ideas, fresh perspectives and an opportunity to learn and understand what you *stand for*, how to *stand out* and what you can do to start building your own *outstanding* brand.

I have applied, and continue to apply, as many of the concepts, strategies, techniques, tools and practices in this book as possible. And I am reaping the benefits by living a wonderful life: I love my work and I'm passionate about it. I am my own boss. I choose my own schedule. I make a decent income. I support my adventurous lifestyle. I work with wonderful people and clients. I am associated with business partners and colleagues who I call my friends. I get to travel and see interesting places. I am fit and healthy. As my mentor and friend Marshall Goldsmith says, "Life is good."

If I – a normal guy from Switzerland who once gave bike tours – can achieve that, I know you can, too. Reading this book and applying the insights will help you get to where you want to go.

Enjoy the journey!

Simon Vetter,
Del Mar, California
January 2005

How This Book Was "Born" ... And What You Can Expect from It

I always wanted to write a book. After I quit my job in August 2001 and became a "free agent," I felt an even greater desire to become a published author. At the time, I knew I wanted to write something about how we develop ourselves, how we fulfill our potential in business and how we work to be the best we can be. I also knew that there are thousands of books in that category. How would my book be different? What would make people want to read my book?

It took me a year to develop a specific concept. In August 2002, I went on a two-week vacation to Switzerland. One sunny morning, I had brunch with my friend and former co-worker Adrian Huber at his house in Zurich. During the mid-1990s, we had both been project managers at ZfU, a management education company where we organized executive programs and management seminars. After a traditional Swiss brunch, we went into his home office for a long conversation amid his personal library. I asked him, "Adrian, what is the hot business topic in Europe?" Without hesitation, he replied, "self-marketing."

Over the next few weeks, I pondered his response and started to study self-marketing for professionals. When I did a search on Amazon.com, there weren't any must-read books that stood out. So in November 2002, I developed an outline for a book on self-marketing. In conversations with friends and business colleagues, I became more convinced that there was a specific need in that area. As I conducted in-depth research in the field, the term "personal branding" surfaced repeatedly.

In January 2003, 40 executive coaches and consultants from the Alliance for Strategic Leadership came together for our annual retreat in La Jolla, California. During a networking session, I approach Marshall Goldsmith with my book concept.

xviii   Stand Out!   Simon Vetter

He encouraged me to pursue the idea and offered specific advice. He said, "Go to people who have developed a strong personal brand, interview them and write up their story. When you have enough profiles, you have a book!" Two months later, I did my first interview with someone who had built a remarkable brand as one of the most recognized authorities in executive coaching. Who was it? Yes, you guessed it! ... Marshall Goldsmith.

Over the next year, I interviewed over a dozen professionals with highly developed personal brands. Eight of them agreed to be a part of this book:

Person	Expertise in
Nido Qubein	Transformational leadership
Tony Alessandra	Marketing
Beverly Kaye	Organizational and career development
Marshall Goldsmith	Behavioral change and executive coaching
David Allen	Personal productivity
Gayle Carson	Entrepreneurship and business management
Brian Tracy	Development of human potential and personal effectiveness
Jim Kouzes	Leadership

Each person is an expert in a specific aspect of professional services: business education, consulting, coaching, professional speaking and publishing. All of them have written books – some a few, others more than 20. They work with individuals, entrepreneurs, medium-sized companies, and many of the largest organizations in the United States and abroad. They teach tools, techniques, skills and strategies in entrepreneurship, personal effectiveness, productivity, communication, influence, management, leadership, sales, marketing and many other areas. Many of those concepts are explained in this book.

In addition to teaching others, these eight professionals apply their concepts to their own lives and businesses. If you do the same, you will benefit in a number of ways:

- You will gain insights on how to make your work more enjoyable, meaningful and fulfilling. You'll find ways to turn your avocation into your vocation.

- You will increase job security by developing your own talent and personal brand. You will learn to attract people, projects and jobs so you never run out of work.

- You will be appreciated and recognized by your peers, clients and others for your performance and excellence.

- You enhance value for your clients and get paid accordingly. Your income increases.

- You will enjoy more flexibility and independence – you are less dependent on others, you choose your own hours and you arrange your life according to your priorities.

STAND OUT! is organized into three parts:

Part one, "A New World of Talents and Brands," is a discussion of the new business reality and the impact it has on professionals like you. I also lay out the framework for talent development and establish my philosophy of personal brand management.

Part two, "Profiles of Personal Brands," highlights eight highly accomplished professionals who have developed distinctive personal brands. Each profile starts with a brief description of the person and their history, then dives into how they developed their brand, what they did to get recognized, their successes and failures along the way, and the key concepts they learned. I conclude each profile with a summary of insights, a synopsis of the key concepts, and specific action steps to explore the concepts further.

Part three, "Personal Branding from Within," sums up what those eight people have in common in terms of personal branding. I also developed a model called "the three building blocks of personal brand management," and include some practical ideas on how you, the reader, can build your own brand. What can you do to develop, build and strengthen your own brand? Where do you begin? What can you do to increase your brand value?

The field of personal brand management is still a very young discipline – only a few years old. However, I strongly believe that with the changing business reality, it will elevate to "crucial" subject matter in the near future. It is – and will increasingly become – an indispensable topic for professionals to explore and apply to their own lives and careers. This book is an endeavor to show you how.

> "Teaching is of no value unless somebody learns what is being taught."
>
> – Tom Watson, founder of IBM

chapter

1

The New Business Landscape

As we forge ahead into a new millennium, society is undergoing a fundamental and global transformation. It's a shift from the production-oriented industrial era of yesterday to tomorrow's knowledge-based information era. This shift is radical and far-reaching – stretching from Helsinki to Cape Town ... from Montreal to Sydney ... across borders, cultures and languages. It's inescapable, and inevitable. You've undoubtedly seen this change in your own life and business. For example, a call to a customer service hotline is routed to a representative in India. My website – an integral part of my business – was designed in Australia.

As a result of this shift, work is changing dramatically – and we must change and adapt to this new information-driven marketplace. We need to take a close look at the economic environment we live in, embrace the new technology, comprehend these changes in society and adjust to them. If we don't, we'll be left standing on the sidelines watching others play the game and win.

> "The rapidity of change has clearly raised the level of anxiety and insecurity in the workforce."
>
> – Alan Greenspan[1]

Job Security is Gone

This economic shift signaled a dramatic decrease in job security. I have noticed that trend in my own circle of friends:

- Cullen Owen, one of my soccer buddies, works for a computer device manufacturer in San Diego. The company was bought by another high-tech company in the summer of 2004. A few months later, they laid off 20 percent of their employees. In his three years with the company, Cullen has survived five such lay-offs and he is wary of sticking around for a sixth.

- Michael Day – who has a stellar resume in information technology – was employed by Hewlett-Packard and telecommuted from San Diego. He was responsible for establishing strategic alliances in the area of networking and Web security. Five months after his company merged with Compaq in 2003, he was fired along with 6,000 other H-P managers and employees. He is now pursuing an entrepreneurial career in Barcelona, Spain.

- Marco Kuna, a friend from Switzerland, was an account manager for Agilent Technologies, a global high-tech company. Even though he was one of the highest performing sales representatives, the company laid him off during a downsizing phase in 2003. Fortunately, he was hired as general manager of a competing company shortly thereafter.

The trend is clear: even strong performers cannot rely on companies to secure their jobs. Loyalty between employer and employee is a thing of the past. Lifelong employment is over.

Big companies accelerate the trend through offshoring: In December 2003, IBM moved nearly 5,000 programmer positions to India and China. GE has moved much of its research and development overseas. Microsoft, Dell, American Express and other major multinational companies have either offshored work or are considering such changes. In just the realm of information technology, the Gartner Group estimates that 500,000 positions may leave the U.S. for lower-wage countries by the end of 2004.[2] Although millions of jobs disappear from the national economy, the good news is that millions of new jobs are created. An analysis of the U.S. economy between 1980 and 1998 showed that 44 million jobs were eliminated and a staggering 73 million new jobs were generated – a net gain of 29 million jobs. By comparison, the European economy created and destroyed 4 million jobs, with a net change of zero. Even German Chancellor Gerhard Schroeder understands the severity of today's business climate. In his words, "Either we modernize or we will be modernized by the unremitting force of the market."

Tom Peters, a world-renowned management guru, predicts the future in a thought-provoking, dramatic and very realistic way. In his latest book, *Re-Imagine*, he writes: "All of our organizations will be reinvented – completely – in the next 25 years. All of our careers will be reinvented – completely – in the next 25 years. All job security, as we have known it over the past three or four generations, is over. Over and gone."[3]

What's the consequence for us, the individual workers? We can only rely on ourselves to protect our jobs. **We must take charge of our own careers and our own destinies.** As long as we remain flexible, adjust to today's business reality and continually update the value we offer to the world, we will never be out of work.

Welcome to a World of Free Agents

There is a broad shift in power from the organization to the individual. More and more people in traditional jobs – the permanent, year-around, full-time, outside-the-home employment arrangement that is the basis of nearly all American labor and social assumptions – are dissatisfied and want to be in charge of their own lives. I declared my own independence by quitting my traditional job in 2001 to become a free agent.

Daniel Pink, author of *Free Agent Nation*, estimates that there are 33 million free agents in America. That is one in four American workers (not including telecommuters). In his book, Pink categorizes them into three groups:

- Soloists (16.5 million): Soloists are people who work for themselves, generally alone, moving from project to project and selling their services. They are independent consultants, graphic designers, writers, carpet installers, computer programmers and other freelancers.

- Temps (3.5 million): Working for a temp agency, they "hop" from assignment to assignment. This group can include lawyers, temporary engineers, temporary project managers and even temporary CEOs.

- Micro businesses (13 million): These are home-based businesses or enterprises that employ four people or fewer.

The following statistics support that trend toward free agency:

- The percentage of workers who described themselves as self-employed jumped from 22 percent in 1998 to 26 percent in 2000. More than 40 percent of Americans have had a period of self-employment at some point during their careers.

- A 1996 study found that 80 percent of independent

contractors preferred working independently, as opposed to being someone else's employee.[4]

- Given a choice between an employee and being self-employed, more than seven out of ten Americans choose self-employment.[5]

- Fewer than one in ten Americans now works for a Fortune 500 Company. The largest private employer in the U.S. is not General Motors or Ford, but Manpower Inc. – a temporary work mega-agency. The dream of America's young people? Not to climb through an organization or even to accept a job at one, but to create their own gig on their own terms.[6]

A prime example of a free agent model is Hollywood's movie industry, where a bunch of talented actors, directors, writers, technicians and cameramen come together for a finite project with shared interest and a clear business purpose. Everyone brings brainpower, creativity, skill and commitment to the project. When the movie is completed, they disperse – each project member having added a new skill, forged new connections, deepened existing relationships, enhanced their reputation within the industry and earned a credit they can add to their resume. Each free agent moves on to their next deal, from project to project, gig to gig, and so it goes.

As Hollywood has gone the way of the free agent, so will California and America. So will the world.

Make Money *and* Meaning

In general, people have had a strong underlying need for meaningful, purposeful work. Abraham Maslow, the famous American psychologist, recognized that deep human drive when he wrote in his journal forty years ago. "All human beings prefer meaningful work to meaningless work. If work is meaningless, then life comes close to being meaningless."[7] In a society in which workers have a level of comfort, work takes on a larger purpose – one that many organizations seem incapable of accommodating. Paychecks and stock options still matter, but work is not just about making money. It's also about making meaning.

People strive for the freedom to follow their own path and purpose. They are searching for autonomy, challenging assignments, setting their own priorities, gaining new skills or knowledge, and defining success on their own terms. That's the work ethic of the new economy. If corporations are not capable creating that environment, people increasingly exercise their freedom to do that on their own. In organizations, people move up the ranks until they stop having fun. Daniel Pink calls this *The Peter-Out Principle*, a variation on the famous *Peter Principle*, which says that people rise through the ranks of an organization until they reach their level of incompetence.[8] The best strategy for managing employees isn't to bribe them, but to treat them like free agents. Lead your employees as if they are volunteers.

The New Bargain: Talent for Opportunity

In the old business era, the social contract of work implied that the organization offered each individual job security – and in return, the individual gave the organization loyalty. The loyalty-for-security agreement that defined much of the workforce during the last century has dissolved. A new bargain, a new social pact, is forming: talent-for-opportunity. Talent becomes the commodity, the most important asset that free agents can offer. The free agent offers talent, performance, skill, creativity, ideas, knowledge and guidance. In exchange, free agents receive opportunities to deliver strong results, manage a fun project, learn a new skill, meet new people, broaden their network, and of course, earn money. Opportunity to earn, learn and connect is the foundation of the free agent market.

The employment market is becoming a talent market. When talent is scarce and the talent market tight, those free agents who offer it will dictate the price. When opportunity is scarce, organizations and purchasing agents will have the upper hand. This market varies from field to field, person to person, region to region as buyers seek specific talent for a defined project with a clear outcome, and free agents seek opportunities based on their interests and capabilities.

Each time free agents secure a talent-for-opportunity exchange, they add strength to their skill base, another project to their portfolio, and they raise their overall value. Consequently, their desirability and "job security" increases as well. In addition, with each additional project, the free agent adds a new client, meets new colleagues, broadens their network and strengthens relationships with mentors. Those combined connections lead to enhanced vertical loyalty, or loyalty to colleagues that crosses organizational boundaries. Pink writes, "Ultimately, the new employment contract of talent-for-opportunity not only replaces loyalty-for-security, but it enhances both loyalty *and* security."[9]

For knowledge workers and free agents, talent is the most important asset. Developing and building talent increases the workers' attractiveness, value and brand. Tom Peters puts it bluntly in the following "rules":

> Talent Rules
>
> Talent = Brand; Brand = Talent
>
> Talent! Now! Period!

"War for Talent"

The market for talent is one of the most explosive, invigorated markets ever. This is partially the result of demographics. By 2020, the United States will have 15 percent fewer Americans in the 35- to 45-year-old range. At the same time, the U.S. economy is projected to grow at a rate of three to four percent per year. So over that period, the demand for bright, talented 35- to 45-year-olds will increase by, say, 25 percent, and the supply will diminish by 15 percent. The stage is set for a talent war.

In 2000, the consulting company McKinsey released a report called "War for Talent 2000." The report is a survey of 6,900 corporate officers, top executives and midlevel Gen-X managers across 56 companies. From the report, the following seven "talent imperatives" are proving essential to winning the "war for talent":

1. Instill a talent mindset at all levels of the organization – beginning with senior management.

2. Create "extreme" employee value propositions that deliver on people's dreams.

3. Build a high-performance culture that combines a strong performance ethic with an open and trusting environment.

4. Recruit great talent continuously.

5. Develop people to their full potential.

6. Make room for talent to grow.

7. Focus on retaining high performers.[10]

What can we learn from that report? Here are four conclusions:

Talent is important, growing talent even more.

We are talent. Since talent = brand, we are brand.

We need to grow, improve and strengthen talent and brand.

Branding is essential.

Facing the Business Reality

Divided into four areas, the following pages summarize the old industrial era and the new information era.

Industrial Era	Information Era
Production oriented	Knowledge driven
What was – in the past	What is and will be – now and tomorrow, present and future

I. Work	
Industrial Era	**Information Era**
Work pays the bills	Work is fun, exciting, meaningful, fulfilling
A job for life; a 30-year career with the same company; lifetime employment	A life full of jobs and exciting projects; learn something new everyday
Staff, employee, personnel, human resources	Talent
Blue collar, "cubicle slaves"	White collar, enthusiastic professionals
Routine, same old stuff, a job	Every day is different, deliver a WOW performance
Do it all	Do what I love, what I'm best at
8 a.m. to 5 p.m., Monday through Friday	Work on my own rhythm, now to then
Retirement at 60	Start a new business at 60

2. Organizations

Industrial Era	Information Era
A bureaucratic, centralized hierarchy	A flat, decentralized network
Steady, slow, stable, predictable	Fast, flexible, agile, virtual, lean
Top-down, command and control	Network-centric, interdependent groups
Units are divided, exclusive, closed	Networks are open, inclusive, connected
Lots of friction, silos, departments	Friction-free, seamless, open communication
Accountants and standards rule	Innovators and creativity rule
Hierarchy reigns: follow the rules	Relationships and ideas rule
Cost centers, minimize expense	Profit centers, maximize value added
Information: "need to know"	Information: "want to share"
Preserve, conserve, "suck up" to the boss	Rock the boat, reinvent, improve
Offices with desk, paper and documents	Paperless office, wireless, connected to the World Wide Web
A safe job with "potential for advancement"	A fun place to work

3. Marketplace

Industrial Era	Information Era
Certainty, quiet times	Ambiguity, crazy times
We deliver good, reliable products that work	We create awesome experiences for the client; we leave an unforgettable memory
Procedure-driven, product-oriented	Client-centric experience
Satisfies a need: "I'm glad I bought it."	Fulfills a dream: "I want more!"
Satisfy the customer – repeat customers	Delight the client – happy clients
Advertisement, commercials	Word of mouth, referrals
Analyze data and present facts and figures	Tell a story and engage the heart
Design is efficient, complex, clumsy	Design is elegant, simple, graceful
Competition	Collaboration, friendship, teamwork

4. Mindset	
Industrial Era	**Information Era**
I am an employee, working for the company	I am a free agent, I am talent, I am a brand
I am satisfied where I am	I always get better at what I do
Learn, remember, keep it, cherish it	Learn, unlearn, change, improve
I do what I get paid to do	I excel and give my best every day
If it's not broke, don't fix it	If it's not broke, let's make it better
Play it safe, defense	Let's take risk, offense
Blame, criticize, judge	Appreciate, praise, show compassion
Change others	Change myself

Source: Tom Peters, Re-imagine! (Dorling Kindersley Publishing, 2003)

The shift to a world of free agents is also a shift to increasing personal responsibility for results. Fostering talent and generating results with passion and enthusiasm is the new paradigm to embrace. While the industrial era laid the foundation for today, the information era and the age of free agents is the path of the future.

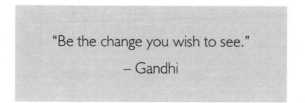

"Be the change you wish to see."

– Gandhi

Personal Branding Philosophy

Everybody has a brand!

Whatever we do, we leave an impression. We send out signals all the time. It's like walking through fresh snow. We cannot hide the footprints behind us. People around us – at work, at home, in the gym, at a restaurant – see and observe us. Our brand is based on the experience people have with us. Every action, every word, every element of our appearance is noted, recorded, and judged by everyone we meet. Ultimately, we always leave a mark. At the same time, this is the process of building a brand.

We have a choice: we can either leave the brand-building process to chance, hoping that people will understand the message we express, or we can take charge and consciously craft the message we want to send. Either we choose to develop our own brand, or our brand is developed for us.

My intention for this book is to raise awareness; to encourage you to be conscious of your actions, your behavior, the impressions you leave and the impact you have on others. Ultimately, it's how you are perceived that lays the foundation for your brand. You must understand what you value, what makes you tick, gives you a kick, what you care about and how you communicate with the world. It comes down to the simple, yet complex question: "Who am I?" The more you appreciate who you are (your identity), what you stand for (values), what gets you excited (motivation) and what you do (behavior), the better prepared you are to proactively develop an outstanding brand.

I have read many books on the subject of marketing and branding during the process of writing this book. One of my favorites is *The New Brand World* by Scott Bedbury. The author, who was the architect of two of the most successful brands in recent years, Nike and Starbucks, describes eight powerful principles in branding. In his role as advertising manager and branding specialist, he experienced both dramatic successes and tremendous failures in brand creation. His knowledge and expertise on branding applies not only to big corporations, but to individuals as well. Scott Bedbury sums up the very nature of branding like this:

> "Great brands are about who we are – how we communicate ouressence, our character."
>
> – Tom Peters

"We are defined by the experiences and actions of our lifetime. So are brands. A great brand is a story that's never completely told. A brand is a metaphorical story that connects with something very deep – a fundamental appreciation of mythology. Stories create the emotional context people need to locate themselves in a larger experience. Every brand has at its core a substance that gives it a strength. You have to understand it before you can grow it. Building a brand is the most challenging, complicated, and painstaking process that a company (person) can embark on. It's more intuitive than analytical, and most of the time it can't be seen. But it can always be felt."[1]

My definition of a personal brand

Often times, people confuse branding with marketing and promotion. Branding is more than creating a marketing campaign, designing a fancy logo, creating a 30-second elevator speech, coming up with a slick slogan, producing a colorful brochure, or executing a direct mailing package. Those promotional tools are important and, if well implemented, can create high visibility. But branding is a much larger task. It has to do with identifying individual uniqueness, creating an aura about your identity, tapping into your potential and making something meaningful.

From studying the field of personal brand management, I developed the following definition:

A personal brand is the Essence of YOU,
as recognized by others.

The definition implies three things. First, it means that you have clarity about the Essence of YOU; your motivation, talents, passion, desire, calling, background, experience, interests and specialization.

Second, you know and have defined who the "others" are. Who is your client? What niche or market are you in? Who are the ultimate beneficiaries of your service?

Finally, it means that whatever you do – good or bad – is getting noticed, recognized and perceived (consciously and unconsciously). Because perception determines reality, other people's perception about us becomes their reality. We create reality, knowingly and unknowingly, day by day, action by action.

> What is my mission in life? What do I want to convey to people? How do I make sure that what I have to offer the world is actually unique? It's a matter of whether or not you want to be ... UNIQUE ... NOW."
>
> – Jesper Kunde, *A Unique Moment*

A successful, effective, well-recognized brand has the following characteristics:

- It is more than a name. It stands for something that has substance, character and identity.

- It is unique and different from anything else out there.

- It is well understood by your target group and clients.

- It attracts people, clients, projects or money to you.

- It is built over years and endures over years.

When a person builds a powerful brand, it gives that person leverage. A strong personal brand builds an aura of trust, inspires confidence and increases credibility. It says: I trust you, I like you and I want to do business with you.

A definition of marketing that makes sense ....

There are many definitions of marketing and branding. Finally, I found a simplified explanation that really makes sense:

You see a gorgeous woman at a party. You go up to her and say, "I'm a fantastic guy." That's *Direct Marketing*.

You see a gorgeous woman at a party. You go up to her and get her telephone number. The next day you call and say, "Hi, I'm a fantastic guy." That's *Telemarketing*.

You're at a party with a bunch of friends and see a gorgeous woman. One of your friends goes up to her and pointing at you says, "He's a fantastic guy." That's *Advertising*.

You're at a party and see a gorgeous woman. You get up, straighten your tie, walk up to her and pour her a drink. You open the door for her, pick up her bag after she drops it, offer her a ride, and then say, "By the way, I'm a fantastic guy." That's *Public Relations*.

You're at a party and see a gorgeous woman. She walks up to you and says, "I hear you're a fantastic guy." That's *Brand Recognition*.

Marketing means
you have something important to say,
you say it well,
and you say it often.

Your uniqueness is your differentiator

Any marketing expert will tell you how important it is to communicate the distinguishing characteristics of a product, service, company or person. In real estate, the critical element that gives value to the property is location. In marketing, it's differentiation. We are all different from each other. We each have our own individual story. We are unique. The key is to ensure that others notice and recognize that uniqueness.

My colleague, Tim Sanders from Yahoo!, explains how knowledge workers run the risk of becoming commoditized. In his bestselling book, *Love Is the Killer App: How to Win Business and Influence Friends*, he writes, "You risk becoming a human switch, someone who performs a function that has yet to be automated, but probably will be at some future date.

And there are millions of you out there, you undifferentiated middle managers, you enterprise resource planners, you service providers. The moment some giant software company can sell a program that switches that same switch you do, you're out of a job. You're a commodity that has been replaced by a cheaper one. As business guru Tom Peters says, 'Be distinct or be extinct.' The best response to this threat is to differentiate yourself. The good news is that there's no such thing as a commodity – only a person that thinks like one." [2]

The most important aspect of building a brand: You can extract a premium if you can differentiate your person, product or service. By being a knowledge hub, the center of a vast network, or an exceptional business partner, you create a unique brand for yourself. You're useful, you're likeable, you're valuable. Essential differentiation is about being different in a way that is positive, productive and sustainable over time. Promote your intangible qualities to those with whom you wish to do business.

> "The attention economy is a star system.... If there is nothing very special about your work, no matter how hard you apply yourself you won't get noticed, and that increasingly means you won't get paid much either."
>
> – Michael Goldhaber, *Wired*

NIDO QUBEIN
on
Being Focused

Nido Qubein came to the United States as a teenager with a head full of dreams, a handful of English words and no contacts. He also brought the simple belief that a clear vision, hard work, discipline and focus would make those dreams come true. It worked. Today, the widely acclaimed business leader, author, speaker, consultant and philanthropist not only lives his dreams, he has dedicated his life to helping others seek and achieve their dreams, too.

Nido is the recipient of significant speaking awards including Master of Influence, The Golden Gavel (from Toastmasters International) and the International Hall of Fame. He is also the recipient of many honors, including the Ellis Island Medal of Honor, and he is the founder of the National Speakers Association Foundation.

Nido Qubein has demonstrated his leadership as chairman of Great Harvest Bread Company (with 210 stores in 39 states); CEO of Creative Services, Inc. (an international management consulting firm); corporate director of BB&T Corporation (the 11th largest financial institution with 28,000 employees and $91 billion in assets); and chairman of McNeill Lehman (a public relations and advertising agency). He has also served on the board of directors for 13 organizations.

How has Nido achieved such impressive accomplishments? To put it simply, he's focused.

Excellence is a habit

Nido Qubein is known as the entrepreneur who teaches transformational leadership, which he's been doing since the mid-1970s through consulting, writing, speaking, training and education. It's been an evolving process. He began with just a body of information; then he honed it and improved it. In time, it has developed into a reservoir of knowledge, and then at some point, it evolved into a degree of wisdom.

He came to America for college at age 17. He had 50 dollars in his pocket, and he didn't know a single person. In addition, he spoke very little English. He worked 10 hours a day to pay for college and taught himself English. He learned the language by taking 3x5 cards and putting 10 English words on those cards. He memorized the spelling and meaning of those 10 words. The next day, he would take another set of 3x5 cards and write another 10 words while reviewing the 10 words from the day before. By doing that daily, he developed a habit. Aristotle said, "Excellence is not an act. It's a habit." It's a habit that we acquire through training and habituations. Something that is worth doing is worth doing well. He discovered that good habits are hard to develop, but they're easy to live with. He also discovered that bad habits are easy to develop, but they're hard to live with.

That's how Nido learned the English language: slowly and methodically. The average American has over 5000 words in his/her vocabulary. When Nido was 17 years old, he knew only a few dozen English words. However, he went on to write over a dozen books, create 100 audio programs, and develop 100 videos that were translated into 19 languages for over 70 countries. He completed his undergraduate and graduate degrees in business, and upon graduating in 1973, he started a

> No one can whine as to why they can't achieve their goals or dreams. You have to be willing to work hard enough and smart enough.

business selling leadership material through direct mail. He built that business slowly and surely, then sold it and began others. Today he runs four businesses and serves on the boards of numerous others.

The point is simple, Nido says. "No one can whine as to why they can't achieve their goals or dreams. You have to be willing to work hard enough and smart enough."

Life lessons

Four fundamental principles helped Nido get to where he is today. First, he learned that there are two pains that each person suffers from. You either suffer from the pain of discipline or you suffer from the pain of regret. One of the primary characteristics that a person must develop in order to create a solid business is discipline. We must be tenacious. We must be committed. We must be able to work hard. Most people are willing to work eight hours a day and think that they can succeed that way, but that is a very limiting premise. We have to work hard, smart and with discipline. For example, Nido reads two books every week. Each day he gives himself one hour to study on a topic or area of his interest. He also writes or calls at least three of his clients every day, which supports his commitment to be a conflict-free person. He chooses not to have problems in relationships. Once a year, the week before Thanksgiving, he makes a list of people with whom he's had a conflict or disagreement. He approaches them and tries to resolve that problem and work through it.

He also learned that who you spend time with determines who you become. So, if you want to become successful, surround yourself with successful people. To become great, you must first walk hand-in-hand and side-by-side with great people. He learned that by:

- Emulating heroes, models and mentors.
- Reading hundreds of biographies and autobiographies of accomplished human beings.

- Observing the mistakes of others.

- Deciphering and analyzing the failures that he has had in his own life and extracting from them ideas and methodologies so he can do better next time.

The third fundamental principle is that learning is a continuum. Every single day before he goes to sleep, he asks himself, *"What did I learn today that I did not know yesterday?"*

> To become great, we must first walk hand-in-hand and side-by-side with great people.

Then, of course, you have to learn that you can be creative, but more importantly, you have to be innovative. How can we do this differently, how can we do this better?

He has probably had a million examples of failure. He once invested in a business that he knew very little about. When the economy turned and things got tough, he found himself in an argument with partners, and realized that he stepped into that business because of emotional decisions, not rational ones. Consequently, he didn't know enough to save himself and he wound up losing a lot of money.

> We do all kinds of little things that eventually add up to big things.

Lastly, Nido learned that you must have consistent execution. We have to stick to it. We have to persevere. The tipping point doesn't happen until the cumulative effect takes place; we do all kinds of little things that eventually add up to big things. In business, there are no rose gardens without thorns. There are always things to deal with and to work on.

The biggest influence

The single most influential person in Nido's life was his mother. She had a fourth grade education, but Nido would put her care, dedication and character against 25 Ph.D.'s from the

finest Ivy League schools. She worked day and night to feed
five children after her husband died when Nido was six years
old. She went on to instill solid wisdom and gave very fruitful
and purposeful suggestions, recommendations and guidelines
for living life to the fullest. His mom would say, for example,
always learn from the experts because the experts have their
knowledge in order. If your knowledge is not in order, then
the more of it you have, the more confused you become.
Meaningful change comes from within, so make sure you
change yourself from the inside out. When you do that, you
will find that while every improvement is the result of change,
every change does not necessarily result in improvement.

Later, he learned all kinds of things from many other
influential people, such as business people, industrialists and
community leaders. One of these leaders is William Horney. At
85 years young, he is a man who built a business, is an industrial
leader, a highly respected community leader, and an individual
who understands that it's better to give than to receive. He
understands the basic principals of how to run a business and
how to be a transformational leader. After Nido met him at a
social gathering, they met frequently, talked often and dialogued
about life. They became very close friends. Eventually, William
became the chairman of Nido's scholarship foundation. The
Qubein Foundation gives about 50 scholarships to college
students every year. Through osmosis, observation, advice
and guidance, William molded much of Nido's thinking and
contributed considerably to his ability to be a leader himself.

Meeting the challenge to stay focused

In developing a business or a personal brand, the biggest
challenge Nido sees for himself and others is staying focused.
Focus becomes actually more important than intelligence. If
there's a choice we have to make in life, it is whether or not we
choose to be in focus.

When our life is dynamic, when we have many

opportunities, when we're invested in a variety of avenues, it is challenging to stay focused. Without focus we really can't get much done. We won't be very productive. Behavioral economics says that for every behavior we display, there must be economic benefit. We must get something in return. If we're not focused, we'll do many, many things. Even a good time manager can't be as high a performer or as productive a leader if they aren't focused. When we focus on the most important thing, we find that other small things take care of themselves. Focus is a by-product of purpose. The clearer our purpose in life, the more focused we are on our true priorities. Once we're focused, we know which areas to delegate, which areas to completely throw out the window, and which areas to devote our best resources to.

> Focus is a by-product of purpose.

When we're in focus, our life takes on a new level of clarity. Just as a camera lens focuses light to form a photographic image, our mind focuses our thoughts, feelings and actions to form a clear picture of who we are and where we're going.

Focus leads to balance, which means success

To the question, "How do you define success?" Nido responds with one word: balance. When he is spiritually, mentally, physically, socially and economically balanced, then he regards himself as successful. He's focused on maintaining a balanced perspective in his life. He wants to be socially active, economically independent and progressive, developing spiritually, growing intellectually and physically fit. Although work is very important, each area really matters. We have to focus on all of the things in life that contribute to progress and satisfaction.

Nido implements his philosophy on a daily basis by first understanding what his priorities are, then working according to those priorities – starting with the most important thing first. Putting this into practice on a daily basis becomes habitual. We get into the habit of doing whatever it is we believe is most important to us. The key is to organize and schedule your day and your life in a way that is non-controlling and allows you to delegate tasks to others.

The personal rewards of Nido's business success include a feeling of fulfillment, clarity of purpose, and the feeling that his efforts to make the world a better place to live and work will help him become a better person. He gets a great sense of gratification from his work. The principal reward couldn't be measured by money, awards, connections or by businesses. At the end of the day, we are measured by the people we have helped, the legacy we have left, the stewardship we are invested in, the philanthropy we have exuded and displayed, and by the seeds we planted in the lives of other people so that they can go out and do something worthwhile in their life.

We multiply and leverage ourselves through other people. That is why Nido is so engaged in areas of life that really do not have anything to do with him making money. In fact, they sometimes cost him money. Along those lines, he does a lot – whether it's chairing a $20 million campaign for his alma mater; sponsoring a Thanksgiving luncheon for 600 business executives to remind them of what Thanksgiving is all about (which he's done for the last

> If I were to die tomorrow, what would I most regret having not done?

13 years); bringing famous speakers and singers to inspire and inform them; chairing a United Way campaign; or being invested in his church. Each one of those things brings him a much greater sense of purpose than making money, or claiming high speaking fees, or receiving the Golden Gavel or the Cavett Award, or any other professional achievement.

Clearly, it's about purpose. It's about fulfillment. It's about answering the question, *"If I were to die tomorrow, what would I most regret having not done?"* And since you're not going to die tomorrow, what's keeping you from doing that? Self-interest is a wonderful thing, but enlightened self-interest is 10 times better. Nido quotes William Barkley, the Scottish theologian, who said, "Always give without remembering. Always receive without forgetting." Whether it's about giving in business, giving in life, giving money or time, whether it's giving advice or coaching ... this is what makes life truly fulfilling. If we find the happiest people in the world, we find that they are engaged passionately in something they care about, something that they would do even if they weren't getting paid. That's why they live longer and happier lives, and that is why they are more effective.

Get the client to say "I need you in my life"

Nido is a critical thinker who helps his clients build transformational leadership in their organization. As a consultant, his strongest ability is to guide others through critical thinking to arrive at premises that are based in reason and on sound assumptions, and therefore can help contribute to good strategies. For example, he's the chairman of Great Harvest Bread Company, and he's been able to guide the leadership of that company in building more stores and becoming a national brand. They've taken the branding initiative from brand awareness, to brand preference, to brand insistence.

He worked with another company that was doing about $10 million in domestic sales 25 years ago. Today it's about $700 million. People don't stay in the business – as he has for nearly 30 years, generating millions in fees each year – without really being a sound advisor and without creating bottom line results. The thing that he and his consulting company are always after is getting enough clients to say: "I need you in my life." If they can get a client to say that, they have a client who is committed and loyal. Then they continue to build sound business relationships and trust. Trust leads to reason. Once they have a reason for the thinking processes, they focus on the issues at hand that can best bring the desired result. Focus leads to value and value leads to success.

In the consultant's world, expertise is essential to success. Nido's expertise is in critical thinking and transformational leadership – in helping leaders grow employees that are high achievers, peak performers or terrific producers. He delivers his service through blended avenues of learning – auditory, kinesthetic and visual. He uses the written form, the oral form, the in-person form, and other formats to make sure that the individual learns. Then, delivery includes a follow-up process to ensure that what a person understands intellectually is in fact something that they will apply to get solid results.

The most important competency

For Nido, the most important skill is listening. If you assume instead of listening, you often conclude the wrong things. Listening means you have to hear what the other person says, but more importantly, you have to hear what she or he doesn't say. You listen with both your ears and your eyes. You listen with both your brain and your heart. You listen with both your experience and your capacity to project forward. When you listen, you really listen for someone's needs, fears, aspirations and goals, and then bring forth what you know. Listening is a very, very tough competency. Listening can lead to focus. Listening can lead to reason. Listening can lead to education. Listening can lead to solutions. Most people want to fix the blame. A listener will always aim to fix the problem.

He figured out the importance of listening the same way he's learned everything else. He read about 200 biographies and autobiographies of great people. He also applied a simple exercise: find people you admire, look for the commonalities they all possess, and write down the five features

> Listening is a very, very tough competency.

or characteristics that make them extraordinary. Nido found that each person has some unique attributes and some common attributes. One pattern that all of these extraordinary people have is that they are good listeners. Consequently, he concluded that listening must be a vital skill to possess.

Nido focused on acquiring that skill. When watching television, for example, he'd listen to what the broadcaster said and then when the broadcaster finished saying a sentence or two, he would mute the television and repeat out loud what the broadcaster just said. He'd do it again and again and again. In a meeting, for example, he would listen to what someone said and before responding, he would attempt to summarize what he thought that person said. He made listening an active process. He did profiles to learn about the different kinds of listeners, like the appreciative listener, the comprehensive listener, the evaluative listener, the discerning listener. He would try to figure out what kind the other person was and how to engage the person most effectively.

Like any activity, listening is a discipline. Remember, it's about discipline or regret. Life doesn't give us what we need. Life gives us what we deserve. We have to focus on a habit. It's the same way he learned English with 3x5 cards. It's the same way he learned quotations, by writing them down, carrying them around, looking at them 10 times a day. If we want to focus on listening, then with every person we talk to we have to really listen – to their name, to what they say – and we must be able to repeat what they said back to them. And then we find that excellence is becoming a habit; it's not an act.

> The best way to be interesting is to be interested.

Albert Hubert once said, "One machine can do the work of 50 ordinary people, but no machine could do the work of one extraordinary person." Extraordinary people always are very good listeners. That's why we find them interesting. The best way to be interesting is to be interested. Part of being interested is being attuned to what the other person is saying to us, not only verbally, but what they are saying nonverbally as well.

Positioning versus promotion

Nido doesn't really *promote* – he *positions*. It doesn't matter how much we know or what we can do. What really matters is what other people believe and perceive we can do for them. Nido wants his personal brand to stand for value. As a result of knowing him or doing business with him or being engaged with him, people benefit in a very valuable way – value based not on how he defines it, but on how the other person interprets it. Essentially, he positions himself as a problem solver, a solution provider, a critical thinker who can guide his clients to the microcosmic essence of the issue and then gently help them arrive at conclusions that make sense. He provides a clear vision, a solid strategy, practical systems and consistent execution.

To be more specific, Nido positions himself as a resource of value in numerous ways. He connects with his clients frequently. He works from a list of 100 of his most important contacts, and once a month they receive something from him. He employs the generosity factor. If he sees a book that he likes, he might buy 10 copies of it and send it to his clients. He participates actively in his community, and he has been the trustee of probably a dozen organizations. He's on the board of all three of his alma maters as well as the University of North Carolina at Chapel Hill. He engages in philanthropy and stewardship, and sends the message to others about what is really important to him. He's the founder of the National Speakers Association (NSA) Foundation, and even has an NSA award of philanthropy named for him. He also donates at least 20 percent of his income each year.

While that doesn't sound like positioning, it actually is. Take his definition of success: balance. He wants every piece of his life to execute itself according to the way he lives his life. Ironically, all of these pieces position him, all of these pieces promote him, and each piece creates what he calls relational capital. There are four kinds of capital: (1) financial capital, (2) reputational capital, (3) educational capital, and (4) relational capital. The more people we know, the more circles of influence we engage in. Somehow, in some way, the universe has a way of taking care of us. Nido gets his enormous referral circle working for him. All of his business comes from referrals. He strongly believes that when we do good, somehow good comes back at us.

> What really matters is what other people believe and perceive we can do for them.

He has a very, very full plate, but it's all purposeful, useful and meaningful. He has intentional congruence working for him. All of the things on his plate interrelate with each other. They feed into each other. They propagate each other. There is leverage and synergy working for him, and the results end up being tremendous.

Personal branding tips

First and foremost, you have to extend *genuine value*. Clients will pay attention when you help them get what it is they want from life. The number one thing is to be valuable – to ensure that results are created when people do business with you.

Second, you must be *authentic*. Authenticity is significantly greater than charisma. While being charismatic and dynamic are wonderful traits, being authentic is precisely what the world expects of you. Another big piece of authenticity is congruence. If you have congruence in your life, then what you say, how you think, and the way you act comes together to make a complete picture. What matters even more than what you do is who you are. The state of being leads to the state of doing. You have to "be" before you can "do." That's what authenticity is all about. It's comes from within the person.

Third, be a *disciplined worker*. Figure out which parts of the day are the most creative hours for you. For example, early in the morning is Nido's most creative time. That's when he does his best writing and thinking. He reserves the afternoons for meetings because it's a less productive time for him. That discipline is a big point, especially for the self-employed professional. Entrepreneurs have no boss watching over them to make sure they are getting the job done. They have to be their own boss. They have to supervise their own behavior. Part of that discipline is a belief in behavioral economics, that every behavior you display must produce economic benefit.

Personal brand management is a discipline

Personal branding means you've got to tell people who you are, what you do, and why your service is better than, different from or more special than your competitors' service. It is about your uniqueness, your differential advantage or your unique selling proposition, and it's about you being a real person. Personal branding is about how other people perceive you. It's about shaping the first thing they think when your name pops up.

> Personal branding is about how other people perceive you as a real person.

Nido has a brand. He wants his name to be associated with the image of an immigrant entrepreneur who came here with nothing, and went on to build wealth and significance in his life. He wants to be remembered as the man who helps other people, who teaches other people how they can be transformational leaders and build better companies, and grow better people, and make better contributions to the world.

Eight Insights from Nido Qubein on Being Focused

1. Having a focus is a by-product of purpose. The clearer your purpose in life, the more focused you are on the areas that really have priority in your life.

2. Good habits are hard to develop, and they're easy to live with. Bad habits are easy to develop, and they're hard to live with.

3. Something that is worth doing is worth doing well.

4. Always give without remembering. Always receive without forgetting.

5. Extraordinary people always are very good listeners. Make listening an intentional focus of habit.

6. It doesn't matter how much you know or what you can do. What really matters is what other people believe and perceive you can do for them.

7. Our state of being leads to our state of doing. We have to "be" before we can "do." Be authentic.

8. There are no rose gardens without thorns. When things get tough, the tough get going. Consistently execute, and persevere.

Nido Qubein's Viewpoints

We can't motivate people

"How do I motivate my team to do the things I want them to do?" The answer is: *"You don't!"* We can't motivate people. They are already motivated. But you can determine what motivates them and use this knowledge to channel their energy toward your organization's goals.

All people are motivated

Some people are like water in a faucet. They have the motivation; all you have to provide is the opportunity. The water is already motivated to flow, but it doesn't have the opportunity until you open the tap. Others are like mountain streams, which flow swiftly but follow their own channels. People, too, may move energetically, but toward their own goals. We should make it worth their while to channel their motivation toward the results management is seeking.

People do things for their own reason, not yours or mine

When asking people to do something, we need to illustrate what's in it for them. It could be through rewards and recognition, or appealing to their sense of pride and achievement.

The key to effective communication is identification

When something becomes personal, it becomes important. When our clients and our employees begin to identify with who we are and what we are, good things begin to happen.

The best way to get people to pay attention to you is to pay attention to them

That means *listening* to others, not just hearing them. Listening is active; hearing is passive. If you listen to individuals long enough, they'll tell you what their concerns and problems are. It's amazing what you'll learn.

Pride is a powerful motivator

Everybody is proud of something. If you know what makes your people proud, you can use that insight to channel their motivation.

You can't change people; you can only change their behaviors

To change behavior, you must change feelings and beliefs. You must connect with people, not just communicate with them. This requires more than training. It requires education. When you train people, you just try to teach them a task; when you educate people, you deal with them at a deeper level relative to behavior, feelings and beliefs. (The word education comes from the Latin word *educo*, which means to change from within).

The listener's perception becomes the leader's reality

What they see is what we get. When we speak to a group, they don't respond to what we say; they respond to what they understand us to say. When others observe our behavior, they respond to what they perceive us to be doing.

We all judge ourselves by our motives; but we judge others by their actions

Put another way, we're inclined to excuse behavior in ourselves that we find unacceptable in others. When our employees are late for work, it's because they're irresponsible and have no interest in their jobs. When we're late for work, it's because we were attending to necessary details that had to be taken care of. When team members engage in undesirable behavior, we shouldn't try to assess motives or change them. Just deal with the behavior. We can't change the motives of our employees, but through positive or negative reinforcement you can affect their actions.

And finally...

Nothing can add more power to your life than concentrating all your energies on a limited set of targets. [1]

Simon Says:

To watch a sample video of Nido's dynamic presentations, go to www.nidoqubein.com and click on Audio/Video Clips.

Read *How to Be a Great Communicator – In Person, on Paper, and on the Podium* by Nido R. Qubein.

Those who learn to communicate effectively with people at all levels, of both genders, and from a variety of cultures and backgrounds will be the pacesetters. Your power to influence the lives of others is as great as your ability to communicate. This book will show you how to communicate effectively with diverse audiences.

TONY ALESSANDRA
on
Finding Your Voice

As an author, keynote speaker, entrepreneur and business visionary, Tony Alessandra helps companies build customers, relationships and the bottom line. He is a published author with 14 books translated into 11 languages, including Charisma, The Platinum Rule, Collaborative Selling *and* Communicating at Work. *He is featured in over 50 audio/video programs and films, including* Relationship Strategies, The Dynamics of Effective Listening *and* Non-Manipulative Selling. *Recognized by* Meetings & Conventions Magazine *as "one of America's most electrifying speakers," Tony's style and message gets audiences excited. How? He reaches people. He gets across new, important information "with a lot of snap" so people can grasp it, remember it and use it.*

From academia to entrepreneurship

The focus of Tony Alessandra's work is helping people improve marketing skills, selling skills, service skills and relationship skills. To understand his brand image, he did a client survey and asked his corporate customers and the speaking bureaus he works with what they think of "Tony Alessandra." Over and over, they describe him as knowledgeable, highly entertaining, approachable, friendly and charismatic.

When he went through his doctoral program from 1973 to 1976, one of his professors was Dr. David Schwartz – author of *The Magic of Thinking Big* and a very polished presenter. Dr. Schwartz became one of Tony's primary mentors and he had a significant influence on Tony's speaking career.

After he completed his Ph.D. in marketing, Tony became a college professor, teaching marketing for several years. When business people in the community would call the university with marketing and sales-related problems, Tony would field some of those calls. This was the seed of his sales-training and consulting practice.

Tony left the academic world in December 1978, and in January 1979 his first book, *Non-Manipulative Selling*, was released. That became his calling card, his business credential, and the beginning of his branding journey. Granted, it was an expensive calling card, but it showed that he was a published author, an expert in sales and a former college professor who had experience in the business world. This key product helped him transition from the academic world into the entrepreneurial world.

From the beginning of his entrepreneurial journey, everything he did revolved around building his brand. He named his company Alessandra and Associates, and he always used the tagline "Dr. Tony Alessandra" or "Dr. Tony." Over the years, the name became widely recognized as someone with a solid reputation as a business expert and speaker.

Find mentors along the way

Three men played significant roles in Tony's career: David Schwartz, Bill Gove and Jim Cathcart, who was Tony's business partner for a several years. David Schwartz opened his eyes to professional speaking. Prior to that, Tony didn't even know that one could make a career by speaking.

Bill Gove helped shape Tony's speaking style – which has become one of his true differentiating factors, his unique competitive edge in the marketplace. Tony recalls something Bill told him back in 1982. "Bill Gove pulled me to the side and told me that my presenting style was too 'professorial.' He taught me to let more of my New York City, playful, Italian background come out in my speaking. That was a pivotal moment. When I started to let that happen, it was a turbo-charge to my career and the development of my character. I wasn't sure what my style was before that point, but now it's very distinct. People know me as the New York Italian, the guy who's in your face ... not in a confrontational way, but a friendly way."

> Letting my New York City, playful, Italian background come out in my speaking was a turbo-charge to my career and development of my character.

Jim Cathcart worked with him on the business of speaking, teaching him to understand it and approach it in a professional way. He taught him to pay special attention to the preparation phases of speaking: planning his speeches in advance, doing extensive audio/visual/staging checks, and doing an extensive post-speech analysis for continuous self-improvement.

These mentors each contributed crucial pieces to who Tony is and how he is perceived in the business world today.

Publish – produce – promote

Fortunately, Tony never had much trouble finding clients. He was "Dr." Tony Alessandra and he had a book. It probably wasn't until 1987, when his first video demo came out, that people really started to see who he was and recognize his unique style.

Publishing proved to be a primary vehicle for his brand development process, ensuring visibility and a consistent marketing presence. He contributed to numerous publications, wrote more books, and recorded audio learning programs with Nightingale-Conant, one of the leading providers of personal development material. He served as a mentor to many people within the National Speakers Association and developed a solid reputation in that circle. He wrote hundreds of articles and began sending out a weekly newsletter to over 100,000 people. Again, the tagline read "Dr. Tony Alessandra."

Tony has since slowed down. He doesn't write as much anymore, though he still sends out his weekly e-zines. He continues to speak, although he's refined his schedule to 36 speeches a year, down from over 100 speeches a year. He also produces one audio album every other year with Nightingale-Conant, and he's created e-books from all of his published books.

He often speaks at events put on by the National Speakers Association, just to make sure other speakers remember him. He writes strategic articles for speakers' magazines, just to keep his name out there. He specifically targets speakers so he can leverage his influence: while he can reach business people, he can have a bigger impact when thousands of speakers hear his words of wisdom, and then go out and use his material, crediting it back to Tony Alessandra. Now, he has this army of people reaching thousands of their clients each year

> Tapping into other people's network and client base is powerful leverage.

with his name and message. It's powerful leverage.

He encourages people to use his material in their books, articles, and speeches as long as they say, "... as Dr. Tony Alessandra says ...." Many speakers, writers and trainers discourage people from borrowing their material, but Tony supports it, as long as they credit him.

The Platinum Rule

From many years of studying the field of communication and persuasion, Tony developed a concept he calls *The Platinum Rule* of personal chemistry and productive relationships. Respect for others goes beyond the Golden Rule, *"Do unto others as you would have others do unto you."* Tony adds an important element to the Platinum Rule, which says: *"Do unto others as they want done unto them."* The Platinum Rule helps us avoid the possible conflicts the Golden Rule could unintentionally set up.

When you treat others as you want to be treated, you can end up offending others who have different needs, wants and expectations from you. The Golden Rule requires that you treat others according to your own point of view. That means you naturally speak in the way you are most comfortable listening; or sell the way you like to be sold; or manage the way you like others to direct you.

The Platinum Rule accommodates the feelings of others. Respecting others means learning to treat different people differently, according to their needs, not ours. The focus of relationships shifts from "this is what I want, so I'll give everyone the same thing" to "let me first understand what they want and then I'll give it to them."

The Rule divides behavioral preferences into four basic styles:

1) Directors, who are forceful, competitive and decisive

2) Socializers, who are outgoing, optimistic and gregarious

3) Relaters, who are genial, stable and eager to please;

4) Thinkers, who are self-controlled, cautious and analytical rather than emotional.

Everyone possesses qualities of each style to various degrees, but everyone has a dominant style. With each of the four behavioral types there's a different way to communicate and delegate tasks to them, compliment and correct them, and motivate and counsel them. You do not have to change your personality. You simply have to understand what drives people and recognize your options for dealing with them. This leads to greater understanding and acceptance all around.[1]

> The Platinum Rule says:
>
> Do unto others as they want done unto them.

Tony's online assessment for *The Platinum Rule* is another example of leveraging your material and spreading your name through other people. For example, if you go to www.BrianTracyAssessments.com, you'll see that he uses Tony's model, noted "*The Platinum Rule* is a trademark of Dr. Tony Alessandra." Brian reaches thousands of people with that site. Tony leverages the relationships of lots of people like Brian Tracy.

Become the best in one area

Speaking has been the cornerstone of Tony's business. His speaking style became so distinctive that it made him set him apart from the crowd. More often than not, when he gives a speech for a group, they don't say, "You're the best speaker at this meeting." Instead, they compliment him by saying, "You're the best speaker we've EVER had." That's his intention and standard of excellence. When he speaks, 19 out of 20 times, he's the highest rated speaker. His speaking skills have helped catapult him above the crowd.

All he did to set himself apart was to allow his New York City, Italian side to fully come out. This is when he developed that charisma he's known for today. In fact, he wrote a book and recorded an album about charisma, to share how he learned to come across ... charismatic, likeable, sociable, approachable, funny and knowledgeable.

Growing up in New York City, he developed a style that many people from New York City have. He calls it street smarts. Tony was a good student in school. All through grammar school and high school, he was an A student. In his doctoral program, he graduated with a 4.0 grade point average. The combination of his street smarts together with his book smarts and natural intelligence merged into a unique style that incorporates the "professor" and "performer."

Tony reads a lot of books, newspapers and magazines such as *The Wall Street Journal, The New York Times, Business Week, Fortune, Inc.* and *Entrepreneur.* He also talks to numerous people every day. He is constantly

> He consistently asks others what's going on in the world and then really listens to what they have to say.

on the phone with people, colleagues, and clients ... really understanding them, their issues, challenges and perspectives. He probes and asks them what's going on in the world and then really listens to what they have to say.

Be out there helping people

Over dozens of years, Tony has achieved a remarkable level of recognition. Experience has taught him what works and what doesn't. Here are three nuggets of his learning:

- Make sure your name is on EVERYTHING: on products, articles, newsletters, e-zines, everything. Create a signature with your name so people are seeing your name everywhere.

- As you are developing your own material, concepts and methods, encourage others to use your ideas as long as they credit you. This gives you a viral effect. This is particularly important to do on the Internet.

- Be a mentor to people because they will spread your word, too. Be there with a helping hand ... always. If you want to build a brand with your name, you need to be out there helping people ... ALWAYS.

He firmly believes in the philosophy of "what goes around comes around." It goes back to the Platinum Rule.

Four Insights from Tony Alessandra on Finding Your Voice

1. Identify and recognize your own style – the essence of who you are.
2. Surround yourself with mentors and learn from them.
3. Build visibility: write, publish, speak and produce. Always encourage others to use your material.
4. Keep your name out there by helping others.

Tony Alessandra's Viewpoints

On Differentiation

Differentiation must come from quality, price or service. Few companies can survive competing on price. This is a monumental challenge that every company faces.

Anytime your customers can't tell the difference between your product or service and your competitor's product or service, the customer will buy based on price. You must be able to differentiate your company, your product, your quality, your service, and yourself if you want the customer to stop focusing on price and start seeing you as a partner, and not just as a supplier. You must show and prove to the customers how you are different.

To find your *Competitive Uniqueness*, answer these critical questions:

- What can I do for my customers that no one else can do?
- What can I offer that no one else can offer?

On Empathy

The root of the word empathy is *pathos*, the Greek word for feeling. *Sympathy* means acknowledging the feelings of someone else, as in "I sympathize with you." *Empathy* is a term for a deeper feeling. It means, "I feel what you feel ... I can put myself in your shoes." Sympathy results in kindness and sometimes pity. Empathy results in actually feeling the pain, or the joy, of the other person.

On Confidence

Having confidence means you believe in yourself, and you trust your own judgment and resourcefulness. To build more confidence, take an inventory of the major and minor accomplishments you've achieved over the past few years. What about the computer course you completed? What about those kids you're raising? Those are accomplishments! It pays to take the time to know your strengths and appreciate them. Confidence is fundamental, and indispensable if you want to engage someone's attention.

On a Winning Image

A winning image starts with a good self-image. A good self-image doesn't follow success – it precedes it.

On Competence

Competence goes beyond having a specific expertise. It certainly means being knowledgeable and skillful in your field. But it also means possessing a problem-solving ability that goes beyond your own specialty. You can choose to behave in a way that exudes competence, or you can choose to undercut what skills you do have by looking and acting as if you're not sure of yourself. Your ability to gain influence with other people is dependent on how they see you, whether they judge you to be trustworthy, and whether they think you really know what you're talking about, or can manage the tasks you claim you can. You'll go a long way toward gaining that trust when you're able to impress them with your competence.

On Vision

A vision is your picture of a desired state of affairs at some point in the future. A vision provides a way for people to agree on goals and how they'll be met. Without a vision, we get lost in the trivia of daily life, or swamped by the feeling of being out of control. Visions are born for all sorts of reasons: to make money, to end a problem, to improve a situation, to create an alternative, to have more fun. Some people have visions where other people see only problems or nothing at all. What would you build on that empty field outside of town?[2]

Simon Says:

📖 Read *The Platinum Rule: Discover the Four Basic Business Personalities – and How They Can Lead You to Success* by Tony Alessandra and Michael J. O'Connor.

The Platinum Rule provides a simple technique for increasing understanding in the workplace, a social setting, or any relationship. The book provides a concept and tools for people to determine their own personality types, and shows how to identify and adapt to the styles of others for easier relationships and professional interactions. The book is simple and helpful for those who want to increase their sensitivity to others and their power to communicate.

BEVERLY KAYE
on
Discovering Your Niche

As competition increases in our knowledge-based global economy, retaining talented people has never before been so critical to American business. Beverly Kaye is a leading authority on talent retention, career development and mentoring. She has authored and co-authored several best-selling books in the realm of engagement and retention, including Love 'Em or Lose 'Em: Getting Good People to Stay, Up is Not the Only Way, *and* Love it, Don't Leave It: 26 Ways to Get What You Want at Work. *She is a popular resource for national media, such as* The New York Times, Time, Fortune, Los Angeles Times, Chicago Tribune, Washington Post, USA Today, *and a variety of professional magazines. She has written more than 40 articles in various trade publications, including* Training & Development, Workforce *and* HR Magazine.

What did Beverly Kaye do to earn a seat at the table of leading business experts? How did she build her business and name? In the following story, Beverly talks about her brand and how she became recognized as an expert.

Collaboration is sweet

Beverly decided to study the field of career development and employee retention while pursuing her doctorate degree. As a former college dean, she had always been interested in the field of leadership and organizational development. Much of that interest stemmed from her experiences with students. She realized that many of these students were brilliant academically, but they often found out the hard way that academic brilliance wasn't enough to help them make it in the corporate world. She became very interested in how companies develop people.

When it came time to write her doctoral thesis, Beverly chose the topic of career development. One incident at the University of California, Los Angeles changed her view of herself and her perspective on career development. She had completed her coursework and had to defend her dissertation on organizational career development. She had selected a committee that she thought knew her, liked her, and would be gentle. She also chose a dissertation approach that was relatively straightforward, clean and easy, as she wanted to move quickly and get it done.

She was shocked when the committee rejected her dissertation and told her to start again. They said that she operated from her intuition, not from a theory base. They asked her to do "phenomenological research" which requires that you develop your own theory. You investigate a phenomenon and collect data. When your theory holds all your data, you've got it. Beverly tried three times, and failed three times. Working with data was not for her, and she considered quitting. Her mom asked, "Why not quit?" After hearing that, Beverly knew she couldn't quit. And then one of her professor on the committee encouraged her by saying, "Bev, if you hang in there, this will be your career development." She didn't know what that meant, but she knew she had to continue.

> I wish I had known then what I know now!

Finally, she got smart. Out of desperation, she asked a friend to sit and listen to her talk about the data she had collected. As she talked, the theory began to bubble up. When she presented her findings, the committee finally approved her thesis and said, "Bev, you got it." The theory she developed became her first book *Up is Not the Only Way*, and it launched her new career in the consulting field.

The experience taught Beverly that her best thinking is done in concert with others and that there is nothing wrong with asking for help. She has used that lesson to grow her business, her practice and her approach to living.[1] The more she talks about a subject and the more she shares with others, the more it grows. She has wonderful colleagues that she can contact anytime when she's getting stuck. She calls them and says, "Think with me on this."

Understand business challenges

Finding and keeping great people is one of the biggest challenges of modern business. Recruiting, selecting, motivating and retaining top talent will continue to be critical for businesses to succeed, and employers have to find ways to help their talented people thrive in the workplace and lead satisfying careers. Beverly identified this need and used it to carve her own niche among today's leading business thinkers.

> If you want to build an inspiring company, you need to inspire the talent on your team.

"I think inspired talent builds inspiring companies," she said. "If you want to build an inspiring company, you need to inspire the talent on your team. It's that simple. That's what I'm about. That's what our company is about. We'll keep thinking of new ways to offer up our brand of medicine – our prescription. That's part of the challenge and the excitement."

Develop unique tools and products

Beverly considers creativity to be her greatest asset and one that she has developed over time. She is constantly asking, "How can we look at this differently? How can we think outside the box? Let's think of a new way of coming at it." Beverly believes that she has developed an ability to hang on to a lot of little threads and pull them together in order to make something unique happen.

> How can we look at things differently? How can we think outside the box?

Her company, Career Systems International, takes a unique approach – it is "tools-minded" as well as "change-minded." When working with a client, they invent a tool or take a tool that they already have and reinvent it to deliver the required solution. For example, while there are a lot of mentoring tools and courses out there, Beverly's team designs "shortcuts" ... something that makes it easy for the mentor and the mentored ... something fun, engaging and very easy for the client to administer. This takes the consultant out of the equation and enables the mentor and student to engage in the process together. The tool becomes a helpful structure. It facilitates the dialogue.

Build brand awareness

While the human resources world may consider Beverly's name a brand, Beverly was not initially aware of that. She remembers one client who planned to put on a program by Beverly's company and insisted it be called the "Beverly Kaye Program" rather than "CareerPower," which is what her company called it. It made her smile and she said to herself, "See, there it is. I'm a brand."

Brand recognition builds up as people begin to use your ideas and products, and tell others. It now happens to Beverly all the time. She meets people for the first time and they tell her that they have read one of her books or used some of her materials. Recently she was talking with someone in a large aerospace company and this person said, "We have a book club formed around your book. We read a chapter a week. We are all excited about it."

> Brand recognition is building when people who have never met you know who you are.

When she was younger, she knew everyone who used her materials. The fact that she has a larger team to represent her work helps her tremendously. It's an amazing sign that 300,000 people bought *Love 'Em or Lose 'Em*. Beverly's company used to be called Beverly Kaye and Associates. In order to broaden her brand, the company changed the name to Career Systems International. At first, her sales team was against the idea because it was her name that people recognized, but Beverly wanted her company's name to reflect the other talent her company had to offer. "The company truly is more than me. Many others also contribute their expertise. Many of the consultants and trainers that I work with deliver our materials even better than I do. My job is to deliver big keynotes or kick off events," she says.

Come to terms with "Who I Am"

The biggest challenge in building her brand was accepting who she is and what she does well. She considers herself a very, very practical thinker, but for a long time, she fought her own gift. She wanted to be more conceptual or academic. However, she found that her gift is in keeping it simple. It took her a long time to say, "Beverly, you just know how to boil it down and help people remember. And that is a gift."

Now she has gotten to the point where she meets people that have followed her work for 20 years or she runs into people that met her 12 years ago during an event where she was a speaker. She's been in the same niche since 1975 or so. Although she never left her specialty, she's been steadfastly changing it ... morphing it ... improving it ... adding new pieces to it. Her work has changed, but it's definitely been more evolutionary than revolutionary. The key is, she has stuck with her original niche, career development and talent management.

With over 30 years of consulting experience, she joyfully declares, "Today I'm working with a team of people that I enjoy and growing an organization that makes me comfortable. I'm happier at this age with what I do than I have ever been before. I think I've come clear about who I am."

Get your name out there: speak and write

Beverly has always believed that you have to be out in the public talking about what you do and giving your ideas away. Since the 1970s, she has been active with the American Society of Training and Development (ASTD) and other organizations. She makes a point of attending conferences not just as a speaker but also as a learner. She can go back in her files and find material from speeches she gave 25 years ago. Every year, she speaks at many different conferences, which keeps her name and brand visible. Whenever she speaks, she always attends someone else's session. She never goes to a conference, gives her talk and leaves. She's always looking to learn something new, and in her field, there's always something to learn.

> She can go back in her files and find material from speeches she gave 25 years ago.

She has also been a successful writer of books and articles. *Up is Not the Only Way* became a classic in the human relations field and has been published repeatedly over the past 20 years. To have a book still alive after all that time is quite remarkable. *Love 'Em or Lose 'Em*, co-authored with Sharon Jordan-Evans and specifically written for managers, sold 300,000 copies. She never dreamed that would happen. Her new book, *Love It, Don't Leave It: 26 Ways to Get What You Want at Work*, targets employees and may sell even more than her previous books.

Keep going

Beverly is always thinking about her work. There is always some new idea that captures her attention. She has a gigantic library of books all over her office, but she probably skims a lot more than she reads. She doesn't make herself read every page, but she'll absorb the main ideas. She never goes anywhere without a book, a magazine like *Fast Company* or *Fortune*, or her "to do" file.

She is convinced that the most important ingredient in a thriving brand is passion. It is to find your niche and create your work around it. It pays to find your passion and go deep within it. You need to develop your expertise around something that truly holds your passion because there's never a true vacation from it. Her passion and craving for learning and developing new ideas keeps

> The most important ingredient in a thriving brand is passion. It is to find your niche and create your work around it.

her energized. She admits, "I'd like to slow down, to shut down at 6 p.m., to relax and sit in front of the television, but I never do. I'm always drawn toward one more project."

Five Insights from Beverly Kaye on Discovering Your Niche

1. Recognize who you are and who you are not. This takes a lot of self-reflection and self-acceptance.

2. Constantly ask yourself, how can I look at this differently? Make a habit of looking at things from a different angle.

3. Develop creativity. Diverge before you converge.

4. Listen to and learn from many different people.

5. Find the things in life that really excite you, that make you feel passionate. Your passion will give you energy and fuel your life.

Beverly Kaye's Viewpoints

If it's to be, it's up to me

Some people are tempted to hold others accountable for their work satisfaction. Most find over time that those others can't – or won't – deliver what's wanted and needed. Ultimately, you choose your career, your boss, your team and your organization. You decide how long to stay and you have the power and influence to improve your work. Accept that responsibility, complete with its challenges, and you'll get more of what you want from your work and your workplace.

Ask and you may receive

If you don't ask, you're less likely to get what you want. It seems so simple. Yet some people hold back. They expect their bosses to read their minds. Don't expect others to take the first step. Don't make them guess, because most often, they'll guess wrong. Be clear. Be prepared. Be collaborative, and then ask for what you want.

Chart your career course

Your career is your creation. So when was the last time you really gave serious thought and time to planning it?

Give it to get it

First and foremost, make sure you're a solid performer (meeting your goals consistently). Solid performers almost always get more respect.

Job Judo – Go with the energy

In the martial art of judo, you use the momentum of the other person to increase your own energy and effectiveness. You build on the energy coming your way. Similarly, in job judo, the key is to build on the energy that comes from doing what you love. Think about what energizes you. Then find a place to invest that energy.

Up is not the only way

Most folks seem to think they need to move out of their current position to develop. This has never been less true. You can enrich your current work by expanding the job, refining your expertise, or finding depth in areas you really enjoy.

Link and build the connection

When Beverly says link, she means teamwork, collaboration, interaction, sharing, information, coordination and networking. All these activities are vital in this high-speed, high-tech, ever-changing world of work.

Opportunities? They're still knocking.

To uncover opportunities in your organization, tell someone you are looking for them! Oh – and make sure that when the opportunity knocks, you not only hear it but are prepared to open the door.[2]

Simon Says:

Read *Love It, Don't Leave It – 26 Ways to Get What You Want at Work*, by Beverly Kaye and Sharon Jordan-Evans.

How long has it been since you've said you love your work? What are you waiting for? For your organization to care? Your boss to go? Someone to hand you an exciting new assignment? More money? *Love It, Don't Leave It* is the antidote to waiting. It will teach you how to find satisfaction in your work ... right where you are ... now. The book is simple and helpful for those who want to increase their sensitivity to others and their power to communicate.

MARSHALL GOLDSMITH
on
Becoming Well Known

Marshall Goldsmith is an internationally renowned executive coach and leading authority in behavioral change. He helps successful leaders achieve positive, measurable change in behavior. Recently, Marshall was named by the American Management Association as one of 50 great leaders and thinkers in the field of management. He has been ranked one of the top 10 executive educators by The Wall Street Journal, *and named one of the five leading executive coaches by* Forbes *and one of the most credible consultants in the new era of business by* The Economist. *To date, he has worked with over 60 high-level CEOs. He has been profiled in* The New Yorker *and* Harvard Business Review, *and was featured in a cover story of the London Business School's* Strategy and Business Review *in spring 2003.*

What has Marshall been doing to become well known, how has he created his own brand as one of the world's leading executive coaches, and what is he doing to continue enhancing his personal brand? His story reveals the answers.

Learn from the best

Early in his career, Marshall Goldsmith met Paul Hersey. At the time, in addition to being a professor, Paul was a renowned consultant in the field of executive development. Paul offered Marshall a job as an associate professor, which he declined. However, Marshall did take up an offer to sit in on one of Paul's public seminars for executives. The event was a turning point in Marshall's career. "He was great," Marshall said. "I was very impressed with what he did and I asked him if he thought I could teach his Situational Leadership material." Paul agreed, so Marshall began tagging along on his seminars. Despite having a Ph.D., Marshall was not above lugging around video equipment or setting up chairs to help his mentor. "I realized I could learn from Paul ... in terms of how to communicate with real world executives. I learned more from him than I learned in any of my formal educational experiences."

One day, Marshall got a call from Paul. He was mistakenly booked to speak at two events on the same day, and he asked Marshall if he could take his place teaching a leadership program for a large life insurance company on the East Coast. Marshall agreed, and the event turned out to be his big break. The participants ranked Marshall as the most effective speaker during the two-week program. While the client was disappointed that Paul had not shown up, they could not stay upset because Marshall was so popular. Paul was going to charge the company $2,000 for his fee. Then he called Marshall and asked if it would be okay if he kept $1,000 and paid Marshall the rest. Marshall told Paul, "I'm making $15,000 a year. As long as you pay me $1,000 per day, I don't care if you make $50,000!"

Paul also asked his protégé if he would like to continue teaching his material. Marshall answered, "Let me think about this. I get to meet leading executives. I have a great time. They like me. I am adding lots of value. And I make $1,000 per day? Sign me up, Coach!"

Become an expert in a topic that is not covered

Marshall had been in business for about 10 years when someone asked him the question, *does anyone every really change?* His answer was, "I don't know. That's a great question." With a background in mathematics Marshall realized that there had not been any *real* research done that could answer this question. In most large organizations, there was no measurement tool to show if anyone who attended leadership training actually achieved a positive long-term change in their behavior. There was a *hope* that participants improved, but no real way to measure of long-term change. Marshall began to do research and develop expertise in this area, and decided to start focusing on a way to measure long-term change in leadership behavior.

Marshall's coaching process is unique. His clients – mostly high-ranking executives in large organizations – are evaluated by those who have something to gain by improving the client's behavior. He calls these people *stakeholders*. An important element of his coaching method is to first determine who are the client's key stakeholders, and secondly, what are the key behaviors that the client wants to change. Marshall collects feedback from the stakeholders and shares their views with the client. Then he and the client develop an action plan for improving specific behavior traits and schedule follow-up reviews with those stakeholders who provided the feedback. Almost invariably, the stakeholders report – over a period of a year – that the client has improved his or her behavior.

Another distinctive aspect of Marshall's service is that he only gets paid after his client has achieved a positive, measurable change in behavior. If the client does not change, Marshall does not see a dime. Since change takes time to measure, it can take 12 to 18 months before Marshall is paid. While it sounds simple, Marshall has managed to carve a niche for himself using this approach: "I am not aware of anyone else who did this before me. I developed a very clear mission statement: I help successful leaders achieve a positive long-

term change in behavior for themselves, their people and their teams. In the same way that Paul had become the expert in Situational Leadership, I could become the expert in helping successful leaders actually get better."

Have a clear, specific and unique identity

To develop a solid brand, it's important to have a clear identity and try to make that identity unique. Marshall believes that personal brands such as *I like to help people* or *I can help you become more effective* are much too vague. If you look at his brand, you'll see he has very clear and very specific mission: "Helping successful leaders achieve positive long-term behavioral change." More importantly, this is all Marshall does. "Being able to say 'this is what I do and this is what I *don't* do' is very important," he explained. "You have to be careful not to water down your message by saying you can do 20 different things. Very few people have the courage to develop an individual mission statement because once they decide upon that, they find themselves not doing a lot of things." Marshall decided early in his career that he would try not to be an expert in too many things. He determined which things he was *not* going to do, so when people ask him to do those things, he simply says, "I don't do that." Marshall believes that you earn credibility by being very clear in your mission and knowing what you don't do.

> Being able to say "this is what I do – and this is what I don't do" is very important.

The gap between those at the top of a certain field and those at the bottom continues to get wider. The field of professional services is no different. It is crucial to create what's called a "position." In other words, it is important to have a recognized identity so people know who you are and what you do. That way, you do not have to justify yourself. Marshall knows from his own experience that with a strong

brand, not only will you make more money, you will also have more impact. You are able to work with people who have more influence and more leverage. You can also have more fun because you'll be asked to do more exciting things. For example, Marshall was invited to join an executive roundtable with several CEOs of major companies in India in August 2004.

Be yourself

When *The New Yorker* called to do a profile of his life, Marshall was initially uncomfortable with the idea. "Imagine some brilliant writer following you around for two months, calling your clients, watching you coach and teach executives and then writing an 8,000 word story on your life – which you don't get to read in advance!"

Before sitting down for his first interviews with writer Larissa MacFarquhar, Marshall recalled an unforgettable lesson from Peter Drucker – the father of modern management – who Marshall spent over 40 days with as a board member for the Peter Drucker Foundation. "Peter always asks a great question: 'Who is the customer?'" Marshall said. "I asked myself, 'Who is the customer for this article?'" At first, Marshall thought his business clients would be his customers, but then he decided the article should be for his unborn great-grandchildren. "This was a great chance for my descendants to get to know me – even after I was dead. I had a unique life opportunity. A brilliant writer was going to write the story of my life. If I tried to be 'politically correct' it wouldn't be a story about me. It would be a story about a fictional character that never really existed."

As it turned out, the article cast Marshall in a favorable light and has since played a valuable role in making him known to the world. It showed him talking straight with millionaire clients who wanted honest feedback. It explored his Buddhist beliefs and how he incorporates them into his work. It gave happy glimpses into his family life near San Diego and how he became a better father. And throughout the article, Marshall's sincerity shone through. "Having internal congruence is critical," he noted. "Don't pretend to be something that you're not." This philosophy paid off for Marshall, who said he does not have to prove his credibility or sell himself to anyone who has read *The New Yorker* article.

> I learned to be true to myself.

"In hindsight, I couldn't have fooled Larissa anyway. The article wouldn't have been as favorable had I been trying to be anything but myself. She would have seen right through that. I learned to be true to myself."

Be a friend, not a competitor, of your colleagues

While some in the business world thrive on beating their competitors, Marshall walks a different path. Marshall suggests narrowing your field. A unique and clear brand identity makes it easier to develop a professional network. Why? The narrower your field, the less you directly compete with other people. You're not perceived as a threat to other top people. They have their identity and you have yours. Marshall applies this principle to how he runs his business. He does not view other professionals in executive development as competition. Marshall communicates a strong belief that "unless someone else is doing exactly what I do and charging the same amount, the clients have a distinct choice. Other professionals have different kinds of expertise and different price points. If I believe that they can serve the client better than me, I will recommend them."

As it turns out, this positive approach comes back to him in the form of *more* referrals and clients. About 80-85 percent of all his business is the result of referrals from his professional colleagues and

> I work hard to know the best people in fields that are related to mine.

other consultants. Instead of competition, this approach fosters a friendly circle of professional relationships. "I work hard to know the best people in fields that are related to mine," Marshall said. "For example, if my client needs career or life planning, I might recommend Richard Leider. If my client wants to learn about diversity, I might recommend Roosevelt Thomas. All of these people are the best in the world at what they do. They are also my friends. Why compete? It is almost always better to be friends."

Develop "we"

Associating with other professionals in your field can not only help you gain more business, it can also help you build a strong brand – particularly when you associate with people who know more than you do. Marshall was fortunate at a young age to work with Paul Hersey, one of the highest paid consultants in his field, if not *the* highest paid. He learned a lot from Paul's basic philosophy: keep it simple, know your customer and communicate in such a way that your customer can understand what you're saying. Paul was someone who was very good at establishing brand identity at a time when people in the field didn't have much brand identity at all. He was a pioneer. Marshall once asked Paul, "How can I ever sell anything? Why would someone buy anything from me?" Paul replied that he should use the term "we." Marshall smiled, "I began to talk about things 'we' had done in our organization and the things that 'we' had accomplished. At the time, 'we' was 99.7 percent Paul Hersey and 0.3 percent me. It didn't matter. It was still 'we.' There is no way I could have done this alone. By making me a part of his team, Paul helped me to establish myself."

Another key to building a brand was writing books. In

the consulting field, book authorship carries a lot of weight. The first book Marshall did was *The Leader of the Future*, one of the most successful books in the field of leadership. The co-editors were Frances Hesselbein, Richard Berkhard and Marshall. The Peter Drucker Foundation sponsored the book and Peter Drucker wrote the forward. Subsequently there were four names on the cover of the book and Marshall was, by far, the most junior editor. The editors recruited other famous names, such as Steven Covey and Charles Handy, to contribute to the project. Once the book was in print, Marshall had established his name with some of the greatest authorities in the field of management development.

"Associating with people who had bigger brands than I had really helped me because I was able to gain personal credibility through working with them," Marshall said.

Selling is giving

One of the most important things that people forget in selling is the idea of giving. When he was 18, Marshall was in charge of the March of Dimes Bread Drive for his high school in Valley Station, Kentucky. His high school was one of the poorest in the county. The project required people to go knock on doors, ask for donations and when someone gave a donation, offer bread that had been donated by a local bakery. Marshall decided to use a different technique. He

> Forget the rules. Just give the people the bread.

told his team, "Forget the rules. Just give the people the bread. If they want to donate, fine. If they don't, we're just going to throw the bread away anyway, so maybe they can use it." What happened next was fascinating. His team members gave the bread away. When folks tried to give it back, his teammates replied that they didn't want it. They would just say, "Hey, the bakeries donated the bread. It's just going to be thrown away anyway. We're collecting money to help crippled children. If you would like to make a donation, that would be great. If not, that's fine. Either way, just keep the bread." What do you think happened? People gave *more* money! Why? Because when you give things to good people, they give you something back.

Since then, Marshall has experienced this phenomenon numerous times. During his career, he has had the privilege of eating at many of the top-rated restaurants in New York, London, Paris and elsewhere in the world. He noticed that the best restaurants always give the customer something for free. "The same applies in establishing yourself at the top of your field. Give something more. Give something that isn't on the bill."

When you give good people things, they give back. It's a lesson that has stayed with Marshall. "My thinking is, work with great people and give them things. The rest will take care of itself. If people don't respond to this approach, my strategy is simple: don't work with them."

One of the biggest sales ever in leadership development

There are two ways to look at selling, according to Marshall. One is to understand what the client needs and sell to those needs. The other is to have a product or service that the client may not even know about and sell the product. Either of those approaches can work, but Marshall prefers the latter approach. "Sometimes we spend so much time selling to client needs that we don't come up with creative new things. Most of what I've done has not been in direct response to needs that clients knew they had. I'm always looking for creative ways to come up with something that they may have never considered."

In the early 1980s, Marshall accompanied Paul Hersey on a sales call to IBM. At the time, IBM was one of the most admired and most profitable companies in the world. They arrived at a huge building to meet with the executives, and considering that Marshall's only business experience up to that point was pumping gas at the station his father owned in Kentucky, the setting was intimidating to say the least. "My entire goal in the meeting was not to urinate on myself," Marshall admitted. After several minutes, the top executive glanced at his watch and said, "Well, Hersey, what do you think you can do for us?" Paul replied, "Well I need to know your goals. If I don't know your goals, then there's nothing I can do for you. The executive went on to say, "Well, you know the people at the top are going to be successful anyway and the bottom 20 percent are probably hopeless. So, it's the group in the middle we want to work with." Paul looked at the guy and said, "That's one of the stupidest things I've ever heard."

At that point, Marshall felt he didn't need to worry about looking like a fool anymore. Paul had taken care of that and he figured the meeting was over. The executive looked at his watch and then looked at Paul again and asked him what he meant by that. Paul said, "Look, I know the values of your company. You don't want to write off the bottom 20 percent of your company. I don't think you really mean that. The greatest potential for growth is at the very top. They're the ones who can really help you make the biggest improvement. They are probably the ones who will get more out of a leadership program than anybody else." The guy looked at Paul and said,

> Tell the truth. People appreciate you having the courage to be honest.

"You're right. That was one of the stupidest things I've said. Thank you for telling me the truth." The company decided to deliver the program to 35,000 managers and employees. Marshall had just watched Paul make, what was up to then, the biggest sale in the history of leadership development. That deal made his career. What did Marshall learn? "Tell the truth," he said. "Don't just suck up. Executives get that every day! Successful people appreciate you having the courage to be honest."

Invest in the long term

Many people don't invest in themselves. They want someone to give them something. They don't tend to make the sacrifice and give something to others before they get something back. Marshall recalls one day when he was sitting in his office and his partner, Howard Morgan, walked in carrying a small box in his hand. He told Marshall, "I have a present for you. I had a really great job, but I wasn't happy. For the last several years, you have helped me and I've been very successful. So I have a small gift for you." Marshall opened the box. Inside was a $17,000 Rolex watch. "I had made over $1 million because of Howard Morgan's work," Marshall said. "He didn't owe me anything. I wear this watch every day. Every time I look at the watch, I think of Howard. It reminds me to be generous and to take the high road with people."

Seven insights from Marshall Goldsmith on Becoming Well Known

1. Work hard to get to know the best in your field. Surround yourself with them and learn from them.

2. Find a topic that is not yet covered. Become an expert in that topic. Know exactly what you do – and what you don't do.

3. Discover your identity – then build a clear, specific and unique position around that.

4. Make professional colleagues your friends – not your competitors. Why compete? It's always better to be friends.

5. Always know who your customers are. Relate to them and communicate with them in a way that is simple.

6. When selling, always remember to give something. When you people give more than they expect they will give back.

7. Consider building your personal brand as a long-term investment. It takes many years to become well known.

Marshall Goldsmith's Viewpoints

On Practicing Leadership

The major challenge faced by executives isn't *understanding* the practice of leadership – it's *practicing* their understanding of leadership.

On Helping Successful People Change

People who are successful tend to attribute their success to personal motivation and ability (even if the positive outcome was actually caused by external events or random chance). In a positive way, successful people are often delusional – their belief in previous successes helps them achieve more in the future.[1]

One of the great mistaken assumptions of successful people is "I am successful; I behave this way. Therefore, I must be successful *because* I behave this way." They are often superstitious and may confuse correlation with causality. They need to know the difference between *because of* and *in spite of*.

Successful people can have a hard time "letting go" when their initiatives are not working.

Over-commitment is one of the greatest challenges for successful people with a "can do" attitude. It can be very hard for them to say "no" to desirable opportunities.

On Getting Feedback

Just as employees need feedback from their leaders, leaders can benefit from feedback from their employees.

On Changing Behavior

The most important variable in predicting the increased leadership effectiveness is the leader's interaction with co-workers. Frequency of interaction with co-workers is more important than the duration of training programs or coaching meetings.[2]

Simon Says:

📖 Read *The Leader of the Future: New Visions, Strategies and Practices for the Next Era* by Marshall Goldsmith, Francis Hesselbein and Richard Beckhard (editors).

The book contains more than 30 essays from the world's best business minds, each one offering a unique perspective on the direction of leadership for the future. The reader can put together a detailed and rich picture about what makes a real leader.

📖 Read Marshall Goldsmith's monthly columns in *Fast Company*. Go to www.fastcompany.com to read online or to subscribe the magazine.

💻 Go to www.marshallgoldsmith.com and read the following two articles:

"Changing Leadership Behavior"

"Try Feedforward Instead of Feedback"

DAVID ALLEN
on
Increasing Personal Productivity

Early in his career, David Allen held many different jobs – from teaching karate to managing an auto repair shop to starting a travel agency. Then he discovered and pursued his true passion: education and teaching. Today, David Allen is known as one of the world's most influential thinkers on personal productivity. He offers seminars, books and unique advice on how to keep up with today's fast pace. He is the author of two books: Getting Things Done: Mastering the Art of Stress-Free Productivity *and* Ready for Anything: 52 Productivity Principles for Work & Life. *His work has been featured in* Fortune, Fast Company, The Wall Street Journal *and the* Los Angeles Times.

How did David Allen become a recognized expert on personal productivity? What's his recipe to stay on top of the universal principles in personal effectiveness? What are the principles that relate equally to a 10 year old in school, a soccer mom and a chief executive? This chapter explored how he gets his message across in a way that developed a highly visible brand.

Bridging the gap between left and right brain

David Allen's business, and ultimately his brand, is about personal productivity. He researches, develops and teaches best practice behaviors that allow a person to accomplish more with less effort. He offers solutions to help people master the mental game of productivity by showing us how to manage our mind instead of our time, how to focus our attention and how to create systems that work.

His particular style and brand is a unique combination of both results-orientation and quality of life. When people focus on time management and personal organization, it seems dry and left-brained. David adds a creative, exciting side to the productivity element. He wants people to say, "Gee, I am very productive *and* I have fun with my life." The ideas he presents are a fair balance between the polarities of the left brain (clarity, straightforwardness, directness and focus) and the right brain (elegance, grace, openness and creativity). He calls it "the yin and yang of personal productivity."

He was the "number-two guy"...

David's early professional experiences were entrepreneurial. He taught karate, managed a landscape company, ran a direct sales distributorship for vitamins, sold mopeds, and managed an automobile repair shop and service station in Los Angeles. He was also a chief cook and bottle washer in a restaurant, held many jobs as a waiter and helped start a travel agency. Most of these jobs were to pay the rent. He wasn't passionate about the work.

None of these jobs were in the world of big corporations. Usually, he worked in small start-ups because he knew the business owner. David was a great "number-two guy" for small businesses. He wasn't necessarily interested in the business itself, but he was good at seeing what needed to be done from the perspective of the processes.

By working closely with many different kinds of people in a variety of situations, David began to identify fundamental principles that apply to everyone, regardless of their situation. These principles became the core of what he teaches today. It wasn't a conscious process. It just evolved over time as a result of all of his different experiences.

When he managed a service station a block off the freeway in Los Angeles, he learned a lot about dealing with crises and putting out fires ... literally. From this experience, he learned to write down and then review all the projects that had to be done so he could make intelligent decisions during the day. This allowed him to free up his attention so he could follow his hunches when it got so crazy he didn't have time to think. This became a fundamental principle for him, something that psychologists call "distributed cognition" – keeping everything out of your head because it makes it easier to stay focused. By maintaining and reviewing the total workload regularly, you can deal with crises and ad hoc situations from a more mature, grounded perspective.

> Keep everything out of your head – it makes it easier to stay focused when times get crazy.

For the last 25 years, David has been involved in education in some form. Two major interests came together for him during his career. The first one was his curiosity about high-performance behavior and personal growth. He became fascinated with thinkers who had something to say about universal truths and consciousness. He was very much into self-exploration, which led to discovering non traditional education about human behavior. He became a trainer for Insight Seminars, a personal growth company that grew out of the human potential movement, and he used that information personally. It was transformational for him in terms of being able to clarify what he wanted to do with his life and what his unique skill sets were. He realized that he wanted to be an educator, but not in the traditional form.

Second, he discovered a growing appetite for this information within the organizational and professional world. He noticed that many people were hungry for more effective and productive behaviors for themselves as well as their organizations. He explored productivity techniques that made a huge difference in terms of people's energy, focus and their ability to operate effectively. That intrigued him. He always liked to go into situations, assess opportunities for improvement, enhance the process, make things work better and then go on to the next challenge.

... And now he is his own brand

The many different professions he held, and his experience in running small companies as the number-two person, increased his confidence in himself and his abilities. It was a process of maturing, learning and exploring. In 1981, he decided to start his own consulting company, and began to work with small businesses ... mostly people he knew and had worked with before. From there his business grew one project at a time basis.

A key turning point came when the person responsible for organizational development at Lockheed came across David's material in the early 1980s, and he invited David to work with his Organizational Development team. By conducting organizational assessments, they uncovered a big need in their culture for personal productivity. People needed to take more responsibility and more risks, manage themselves better, avoid pointing fingers, take control of situations and move things forward out of their own initiative. As a team, they designed a pilot seminar in personal productivity for mid- and senior-level managers. They delivered the program to one thousand managers over the course of one year. It hit a nerve. It was very successful, and a pivotal event for David's consulting practice.

David's work has always been very market driven. He

evaluated information and what people needed, and then wove it into a format that was effective. Along the way, he gathered a tremendous amount of positive feedback from people who were able to walk out of his seminars, go back to their desk, and see a huge impact in terms of what they were doing. For instance, he had spent several years inside one of the most reputable global investment banks. It was an extremely challenging and demanding corporation. He taught productivity tools to investment bankers, the best and brightest people in the industry. Their expectations were huge. The cost of taking a day or half day out of their busy work schedule was high. He knew his program had better be good! Sure enough, they liked it, got value from it and rehired him. Delivering a sophisticated program to a client with high demands and expectations was both a tremendous learning experience and a breakthrough.

As David has developed his business, many of the people he has worked with end up leaving their positions to move on to bigger assignments. Once they got into a new workplace, they realized how much they relied on this new way of thinking. They made sure that David was brought into their new organization to work with their teams.

Getting results without stress

David Allen's message is very relevant and timely to people in the competitive environment on online business. We've all found ourselves saying, "I don't have enough hours in the day to do all things I need to do," or "I don't have enough time!" David's work addresses that common challenge in people's business and life. His work is about managing ourselves and all the stuff in our lives:

- How do we manage our energy ... our commitments ... our agreements?

- How do we inventory those? How do we track them? How do we stay focused?

- Where do we get our creative energy? How do we put that energy to use?

He has uncovered some of the best practices to deal with those issues, and that became the hallmark of his message. He packaged these insights into one- to three-day seminars. Participants learned great tools that had a tremendous impact on how they felt about getting things done, on their stress level and on their ability to get results with much less effort.

When people focus primarily on better results, there is a tendency to compromise in the quality of life. He discovered a powerful answer to that dilemma by practicing karate. As he worked toward his black belt, he adopted a core martial arts analogy, the idea that there is a lovely balance between focusing on results and being relaxed. In karate, the power of a hit comes from speed, not muscle power – a tense muscle is a slow muscle. This means your ability to generate results is directly proportional to your ability to relax. You cannot get things done faster until you learn to slow down, take a step back and get a different perspective on how you do things. Relaxation is the key to focus. You must be able to clear your head to focus your energy appropriately. This truly is an elegant model of productivity. Since David had not been a very physical, athletic person, he started to apply that principle of karate to create the largest amount of power or impact with the least amount of effort. Attaining his black belt was significant because it gave him this physical component, which added a lot of depth to his perspective and experience.

> Our ability to generate results is directly proportional to our ability to relax

Responsibility is the root

From David's own life experience, there is one thing that people need to learn in order to increase productivity: Taking responsibility – being responsible for where they have put their energy (their actions in the past) and being responsible for what they are doing with it now (their action now and in the future). We create our own experiences because we are the ones who allow *stuff* to enter our lives. We don't have to go to some universal, cosmic level of that truth to bring great value to people. Just look at the paper that people let stack up on their desk, and there is a great little model about what they've allowed themselves to create and how they have energy tied up. That energy is not available to other things until they know how to manage it, define it and get control of it.

For example, what does your e-mail inbox look like? An overloaded inbox simply represents what you have allowed to come into your world that needs to be managed. Many people have stuff in their inbox that they keep leaving there. They are not dealing with the input they have allowed to come into their life. There's nothing wrong with having more in your inbox than you have processed, as long as you're going to get to it at some point and that it maps your own agreement with yourself. The fact is that if the good fairy showed up and all of your e-mails disappeared, in two weeks you'd have the same number again. It's not about how much you have, it's about your comfort zone and how many unprocessed e-mails you feel comfortable with. You want to be able to

> We create our own experiences because we are the ones who allow stuff to enter our lives.

close open loops and have clear agreements with yourself. This will allow you to be more relaxed when surprises come up. Rather than being stressed, you'll get creative.

Improving effectiveness for knowledge workers

In the field of effectiveness and efficiency, Peter Drucker was one of the first to define the realm of "knowledge work." Peter often expressed that the toughest job of a knowledge worker is to define his or her "work." The work is not self-evident. They needed clarity.

To gain clarity we have to go to a higher place. David knows that clarity is never found at the same level as the confusion. He recommends that people loosen their conceptual grip, let go of the level they're focusing on, shift the horizon to another level and lift your sights. It's just like going on an airplane ride – the higher we go, the further we see. The ultimate task is to define the different levels of our own commitments. We need to gain clarity on every one of the following five levels to sharpen our focus:

- What is the project about? What is my role in this project? – This is the 10,000 foot level.

- What are my jobs and area of responsibility? – Now you've climbed to the 20,000-foot level.

- Where do I want to be a year from now? – This is the 30,000-foot level.

- What's my vision for the next ten years in my life? What do I want to have accomplished in that timeframe? – This represents the 40,000-foot level.

- What's my purpose? What am I really passionate about? – This is the 50,000-foot level.

Most people don't have a clear vision about where they're going and they haven't clarified what short-term things they need to accomplish to make their vision happen. They haven't defined their projects – all of the projects they have or need to set up in order to manage all of their areas of focus and responsibility. And most people haven't figured out the next action that will move these things forward. Too many people don't know why they're doing what they're doing. Just think about the number of projects, tasks, assignments and to-do's people have going at any one time. How do we define

> The toughest job of a knowledge worker is to define his or her "work." Knowledge work is not self-evident.

the 20 to 30 projects as real projects that we need to get done? What about the 100 to 200 action steps that go along with them?

The main point here is that you really have to focus on each of these levels. They aren't predefined for you. That's David's focus: defining the actions that will move you forward in the most efficient, effective way. You have to consciously consider these levels because if you don't, the pressures of life will decide for you. It's like waiting for the mugger in a dark alley before you start practicing your karate. It's too late. Plan your actions ahead of time, and you'll be in a much better position to be effective.

The key questions about the various levels of work have to be included in this productivity game. Defining your work is a much more subtle, sophisticated thing to do than simply applying A-B-C priority codes or making lists. There's a lot more to it than that.

Selling a personality is easier than selling a process

Over the years, and through many failures, David came to the conclusion that it was easier for him to sell a personality than a process or concept. When he was part of a partnership with two or three other consultants, they were selling a process not a personality. He didn't create any kind of individuality around the name "David Allen."

However, as business growth began to stagnate, financial pressures necessitated a new approach. David did some research and found that, at the time, the people who bought his services were a group of about 30 champions inside large corporations. Most of these relationships were ones that David had created and maintained through his personal engagement with them. "David Allen" was becoming the message and the medium. People were buying him and his style rather than a concept. Clients were interested in the David Allen training. He began to realize that he had more equity in his own name than there was in the consulting group's name.

Initially, it was a big challenge to promote his own name because he didn't have the personal style of a self-promoter. He was not comfortable putting his name on the letterhead because he tended to be reserved. Again, it had to do with his ease in being the number-two person. It wasn't a natural process for him to throw himself out there and say, "Hey, look at me. This is really cool!" That skill is one he had to develop over time. He learned to be confident and willing to put the David Allen name on the map, and to create a positive mythology around his name and what it stands for.

He was willing to *sacrifice* his personality, promote it and build a brand through his reputation. It was a lot easier to wrap the brand around a personality than a process.

There was a rewarding consequence that came along with that shift: it gave him the freedom to take his own paintbrush and say, "Okay, here's the style that I'd like," rather than representing a group and compromising with equal partners. He developed his own style and design, a combination of creativity, ease and focus: "make it up – make it happen", the yin and yang of productivity.

His true purpose

At heart, David Allen is an educator. His mother was a schoolteacher, one of a long line of old-maid schoolteachers in his family. He always thought that at some point he was going to be an educator, but he had no idea that it would be along these lines. David's true passion is self-awareness and assisting other people in discovering that. He is driven to improve, expand and grow his abilities to experience life at deeper levels. It has been gratifying to offer education and create experiences for people that allow them to improve their lives in a productive, positive way with little effort.

The book was his breakthrough

Initially, it was a struggle to sell his material from a traditional standpoint. It never really worked to grow the business by hiring sales people to take his material, package it, position it, knock on doors and get people to buy it. What *was* successful was being out there, broadcasting the productivity principles and letting good clients experience the power and impact. He knew he had to leverage the clients' experiences and those relationships. The challenge was to establish the relationship to begin with.

There was no common denominator in terms of a client profile – except that his clients were smart, savvy and moving on a fast track. They wanted their life, both personally and professionally, to be better in the short-term. Those people were attracted to him and his seminars. He couldn't go find them – they had to find him. That was his big "ah-ha." His business had to grow through referrals.

Initially, few people knew David Allen. He had no resources and little capital. The company still had debt. That forced him to focus on getting his message out as broadly as possible. He had to be creative in opening up the funnel and letting those people find him. Although he used different words for this, he focused on creating a brand. The strategy was the website and a book, but the critical *incident* was definitely publishing his first book. He knew intuitively it was the thing to do. He wanted to test his

> Writing a book adds credibility. When we are willing to put things in print, the world can shoot at it – it's a maturing process.

material in the fires of reality and then broadcast it through print. It took four years to get it done: one year to frame the concept, get an agent and a deal with a publisher, two years to write it (writing was not his day job) and another year for editing, publishing and marketing. *Getting Things Done* was published in 2001. It became a best seller and his best calling card. He got great press. *Fast Company* wrote an initial one-page article and then a five-page article on him, pieces that made a huge difference in terms of publicity and reputation.

Once the book got recognition, his daily consulting rate quadrupled. Interestingly, as soon as he put anything in print, people would automatically think it was the truth. A book builds tremendous credibility. He laughs about it. "When we are willing to put it in print, the world can shoot at it – it's a maturing process. It's like getting a degree. What we learn at university is not as essential as demonstrating the rigor that we can hang in there and get through it."

Key ingredients of the David Allen brand

David's brand was built from the inside. It took more than 20 years and he is still refining it. He recommends taking a solid inventory of yourself in terms of what is unique about what you do. What do you love to do? Check with the people around you; ask your kids, friends and co-workers what is unique about you. Be willing to put yourself out there and give yourself a visual image.

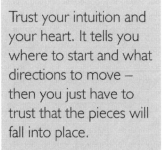

Trust your intuition and your heart. It tells you where to start and what directions to move – then you just have to trust that the pieces will fall into place.

A picture is worth a thousand words. Furthermore, he suggests working with a creative strategist, somebody who has a good creative eye and can help you see things you can't. Your image needs to reflect something that you truly want to be – the essence of your personality. Portraying the style and image is like wearing a suit of clothes. It has to feel comfortable. David loves his image. He loves his business card and his website. It is his life expression. That is where some of the power comes from. People sense that congruence. In a way, his image serves as a bootstrap. On days when he feels down, he has to pick himself up and step into his own image.

There is value in creating a little bit of a myth around your name, as long as it is congruent. It has to be you.

David's basic rule of thumb for successful business practices: keep the same phone number and don't mess up. If you can just stick around and plant seeds with consistency and congruency, you can make it. It just takes time.

The real key for building his brand was putting together the pieces of the puzzle with the right people: a great book agent, a fabulous editor, an incredible technologist and web marketer, and a superb creative strategist. He also counts his wife, who has been a major support in building the back end of the business, as a member of his "dream team." The team offers a tremendous amount of love and support for him, and holds his best interests at heart. He wishes he could say, "And here's the formula for how you find the right people." Somehow, they found him – the right people at the right time. Trust your intuition and your heart. They will tell you where to start and what directions to move, and then you just have to trust that the pieces will fall into place.

Five Insights from David Allen on Increasing Personal Productivity

1. Take responsibility for where you put your attention and energy.

2. Our ability to generate results is directly proportional to our ability to relax. Slow down, take a step back and get a different perspective on how to do things.

3. Become comfortable in promoting yourself and your own name. People trust people more than processes.

4. Write and publish – it adds credibility and increases consulting fees, too.

5. Surround yourself with the right people to help you build your brand.

David Allen's Viewpoints

A change in focus equals a change in result

The greatest power we have to affect our world is always at our fingertips: our ability to change how we see things.

Energy follows thought

You are powerful all the time, by way of your attention and intention. The question is, "Toward what are you pointing that power?"

Getting to where you're going requires knowing where you are

A map is not functional until you know where you are on it. Objectively viewing your current reality always reduces confusion and misalignment.

The clearer your purpose, the more ways to fulfill it

There's a fascinating paradox of the material world: The more specific your vision or intention, the more expansive the creativity you will unleash. The more you know why you are doing what you are doing, the more freedom you have to explore all kinds of ways to get there.

Cleaning up creates clear direction

Creativity shows up when there's space. When mental space is cluttered with too many distractions, unmanaged agreements and loops, flow is limited. Closing open loops, whether they are major projects or boxes of old stuff, releases energy. For example, cleaning your garage can be one of the most effective ways to spark a dynamic vision.

If it's on your mind, it's probably not getting done

To get things done, the solution is simple: Write it down. Look at it. Think about it. Do it or say to yourself, "Not now."

Knowing your commitments creates better choices of new ones

Stress comes from unkept agreements with yourself. You can relieve that stress only by canceling the agreement, keeping the agreement or renegotiating it. But you can't renegotiate agreements that you forgot you made. They must be made conscious and kept to alleviate the pressure.

Perspective is the most valuable commodity on the planet

Putting things in a different context can generate unrealized ideas and solutions. Your point of view can change the most drastic circumstances into the most powerful positive experience. An infinite number of things in the universe are held back from you only by your altitude and attitude. Simply put, a change in focus equals a change in results.

The value of a future goal is the present change it fosters

A vision of a desired future allows you to focus immediately on an improved condition. Its value is not actually about achieving something in time, but rather about how it changes the substance and quality of the decisions you're making in this moment. It affects what you choose to perceive, feel and do in the present.

It's hard to stay on track without rails

We don't feel constrained by the limitations that really work for us. We're grateful for the lines down the middle of the road – they give us the freedom to get places fast with a minimum of stress and risk. Effective forms don't take space – they create it. At times, tightening up our systems is what's needed to release new levels of output.

You can't win a game that you haven't defined

Games are fun only when you know the specific goal. The vision of "playing soccer" is realized only with a playing field and a goal at the end. And the activity of kicking the ball becomes meaningful when you know exactly where you want to kick it. The game of work requires the same edges and directions.

Too controlled is out of control

In golf and tennis, too firm a grip can cause you to "choke" a shot. Hanging on too tightly can limit your ability to deal with things from the most productive perspective. Fine points are fine, as long as there's a point.

You're the only one playing your game

You have created, accepted or promoted whatever you are experiencing. That's the great news, because you're in charge and you can change it if you want. Learning to respond effectively and efficiently to everything that has hooked your attention is a masterful behavior.[1]

Simon Says:

📖 Read *Ready for Anything: 52 Productivity Principles for Work and Life* by David Allen.

In 52 short chapters, David provides universal principles for mastering the balance between life and work. It's healthy food for the mind, mentally stimulating, thought provoking and immensely valuable in creating a stress-free, productive life.

GAYLE CARSON
on
Making Things Happen

Gayle Carson, known as the "Wiz of Biz", is a writer, speaker and consultant specializing in business management, communication, marketing and customer service. She holds a doctorate in education, and is a certified speaking professional and a certified management consultant. Her entrepreneurial career has included a talent agency, a chain of career schools, a convention service business and a real estate investment firm, which she runs with her husband. Her book, Winning Ways: How to Get to the Top and Stay There, *has sold more than 50,000 copies. With over 45 years of business experience, she has worked with a thousand different clients in 50 different industries, across 49 states and 50 countries.*

For her entire adult life, her mission has been helping others "be the best they can be." While building her businesses and raising three children, she has always given her best – despite many obstacles and challenges. Here is her story on how she has made it happen.

Being a young business owner

Gayle Carson was born in Albany, New York, and graduated from Emerson College in Boston, Massachusetts, with bachelor's degrees in English and theater. She always liked stage performing, singing and dancing. Shortly after graduation, she moved to Miami with a dream. She went to work in a modeling school. Within two weeks, she got the job she wanted. Only eight months later, at age 21, she bought the school and was in business on her own.

When she started her business, she didn't really think about the challenges as a business owner. "I was so young and so naive that I didn't know to be scared," she said. "It just never occurred to me that I would fail. Everybody told me I was too young and that I should not move away from home. Remember, this was the 1950s and there were not many women in business. I never thought about these things. I just thought, I'm going to do it. I was not aware of the disadvantages or stumbling blocks at all." When she was president of the Modeling Association of America, she had the opportunity to put the first *Model of the Year* pageant on television. Although she wasn't sure how to do it, she just walked into a PR agency without hesitation or doubt. She sold it to them, and they then sold it to the Wide World of Entertainment, which aired the show on ABC at 11:30 p.m. She had Barbara McNair and George Hamilton as host and hostess.

> Everybody told me I was too young and that I should not move away from home. It just never occurred to me that I would fail. I just did it.

Over the next 20 years, she developed her business into a chain of career schools, which included fashion merchandising, court reporting, legal and medical secretarial programs, real estate and travel, as well as modeling and personal development. She also built the largest talent agency in the State of Florida to be licensed by the Screen Actors Guild and the American Federation of Televisions & Radio Artists. They offered services for print, TV commercials, movies and conventions. She built a company with seven divisions and multiple locations, and managed over 350 people.

As she has matured, there have been more stumbling blocks because she is more conscious of what can go wrong. Now it's a feeling of looking before taking a leap. She still leaps (i.e. takes risks), but she looks a little more. During the beginning of her career, she didn't look at all. She just did it.

Transitioning into professional speaking

In the early 1980s, when she had the convention service company, she was part of Meeting Planners International – now called Meeting Professionals International. She was president of the South Florida Chapter and a member of the board of directors, so she knew a lot of people in the association and convention business. Speakers at those events repeatedly told her about the National Speakers Association and recommended that she get involved. When she joined, she discovered that she could make a living with professional speaking, so she decided to sell her companies and transition into the speaking profession full time. At the same time she became a keynote speaker, she was completing her doctorate in education.

To get her speaking career started, she got out her meeting planner directory and started with the A's, making 100 calls a day. On average, she reached about 33 people for every 100 calls, sent out 10 information packets, and from those 10 packets would get maybe one booking. It took her about nine months for the cycle to start, then she would average between 100 and 150 engagements a year. What makes her so effective is her attitude towards rejection. She doesn't believe in it and says with conviction, "Well, there's only two things people can say: 'yes' or 'no.' So it's a 50/50 shot. I don't care about those that say 'no.' I only care about those that say 'yes.' I'll call anybody about anything if there is an opportunity."

For 20 years she did speaking and consulting, developed a line of books and audio resources, and delivered a lot of training programs for companies. She became best known for customer service, leadership, team building and interpersonal communication. It was always in the soft-skilled areas of getting people to do a better job at whatever they did. That's when clients started to call her "The Wiz of Biz." She has worked with entrepreneurial and medium-sized businesses, and has showed them how to make more money by improving their workflow processes and getting their people to work together as a team. She calls it the "ROI factor" – which is having the right people in the right job, with the right workflow processes and the right communication culture. That's what she's good at, and that's what she's known for.

> People can say 'yes' or 'no,' that's a 50/50 shot. I don't care about those that say 'no'. I only care about those that say 'yes.'

Gayle also became a certified trainer for Tom Peters. Tom had a license agreement with Career Track and she was one of 19 trainers to teach the *In Search of Excellence* program.

Credibility comes from a strong performance record

Her Unique Selling Proposition (USP) is that she is the only woman who has been in business for 45 years; has a doctorate degree in education, a CSP (Certified Speaking Professional) and a CMC (Certified Management Consultant credential); and has served 1,000 different clients in 50 industries, 49 states and 50 countries. Nobody else can say that. Boiled down, it's nothing extraordinary except that she has been successful in business for a long time. It's a combination of her practical experience, the real world savvy and the intellectual value of her education. It's her track record that distinguishes her from others.

In addition, her tremendous energy level makes her unique. She is a fitness and health fanatic who devotes two hours every single day to her workouts. Whenever possible, she takes kickboxing and step aerobics classes six days a week, with a little bit of floor work and weight training. In addition, every other day she either hops on the bike or the treadmill. On Sundays, she walks five miles on the boardwalk at the beach. To make it more productive she changes her workout routine every 30 days.

Gayle's workouts allow her to stay fit and energized, get rid of stress and avoid getting colds, flu and other illnesses. It also helps her feel better about herself. It's hard to believe she is in her sixties. "I run around as if I'm 25," she said. "I do so many things in a day; I'm up and I'm down, and I bend and I lift and I pull – I just don't consider myself an elderly person but I know that probably everybody else does. I really am that age but I don't feel it and I don't think I look or act that way." It's that kind of perception and self-image that keeps her active and vigorous.

Whatever happens, learn to deal with it

Her sister, a psychotherapist, once asked Gayle, "Where do you get that energy and enthusiasm?" She responded: "I've just always had it. I was in my first dancing recital when I was three years old. I did a somersault, my crown fell off, so I put it back on but it was backwards. The audience started to laugh. My mom told me to stop, I put my hands on my hips, waited for the audience to stop laughing and then asked the piano player to start again and I finished my dance."

When Gayle was 13 years young, she didn't want to baby-sit like all her friends. Instead, she got a job selling Avon cosmetics door to door. She became the top sales person in the whole area! Gayle has fond memories of that job: "It was a great time. It was the 1950s, people were home, and they would let me in. I would sit down on their couch and I refused to get up until they bought. They really didn't know what to do with me, so they ordered. When I get something in my head that I want to do, I go out and do it. I don't know what that is. It's just a drive that I have."

> When I get something in my head that I want to do, I go out and do it.

She learned about discipline and persistence from her mother, who expected a lot from her. "You always had to go out with the first boy that asked you because you just didn't turn someone down. And whatever project you started, you had to finish. You didn't come home with B's and C's. You came home with A's because it was expected. You said 'thank you' and 'pardon me' and 'excuse me' and you treated people right no matter who they were. You treated them fairly and equitably and that's the way it was. That's how I was raised."

She remembers her first year of college, at Syracuse University – she hated it there. She went with her dancing partner to audition for a show. She had taught him dancing. The director asked if they would split up and he said no. Gayle said yes because she thought they wanted her. It turned out they wanted him, because there were no male dancers available. Gayle was devastated. Crying, she called her mother who said, "Wake up, this is college, this isn't the real world. If you can't take it here you won't be able to take it out there. So just deal with it, get on with your life and forget about it. You are going to stay there for the year and at the end you can transfer where you want." That's the way it was. Whatever happened, she learned to deal with it.

Gayle has learned to overcome difficult situations. No matter what has happened or how business has changed or what traumas have happened in her life, she survives and goes on. "I'm a three-time cancer survivor and I don't think while I was going through it anybody even knew about it," she said. "I would go in for my radiation treatment at 8 a.m. and get on a 10 a.m. plane, go give a speech, and fly back that night and then be in the hospital at 8 a.m. the next morning. I did that for five or six weeks. I had eight surgeries in two years, but I just keep going. The doctors said they had never seen anyone heal as fast as I did or have the attitude I did. Everybody called me 'Little Miss Sunshine' because I would come in for my treatments and have a smile on my face and everybody else was depressed. I was getting cured and that was the most important thing."

> Life is not fair. Life is not easy and you need to be able to deal with it. Everybody that you think may have it easy, doesn't.

Bottom line, nothing is ever assured. Gayle's positive attitude seems to have carried her through challenging times without too much problem. She experienced the fact that life is not fair. Life is not easy and you need to be able to deal with it, she says. Everybody on this planet has a story. Everybody that you think may have it easy, doesn't.

Have goals and believe in them

Gayle has always believed in her goals. She writes them down regularly. For example, she always wanted to have a house in Southern California. She wrote that goal on a small piece of paper and kept it on her telephone for 10 years. She didn't exactly know where it would be, but she figured San Diego, Newport Beach or Dana Point. Then circumstances came together and she was going to buy a business in San Diego. Although the purchase of the business fell through, she ended up with a second home in San Diego. She thinks that sometimes circumstances just throw you into where you are supposed to be. When my son told his friends that we bought a place in San Diego, all of his friends said, "Oh, your folks wanted to be out there for years."

Strangely enough, even though she had written goals, she never wrote a business plan on paper. She had it in her head and always knew what she wanted to do and how to do it – but she didn't write it down. Although you need a business plan if you go to a bank for a loan, she had never applied for financial assistance. She has always operated on whatever money she had and never worried about it. Looking back, she admits that she really didn't plan well. "I would be much more cognizant of what I needed to do for positioning today. I was just so young and so naive that I believed – I just believed. I went ahead in doing what I had to do and didn't think much more about anything else. I didn't do a great deal of planning. I would certainly plan now, and look further ahead. I wouldn't go on blind faith."

Get exposure for what you offer

Gayle knows the critical importance of marketing and promotion, and sees that as a process of consistently executing a mix of different tools: networking, speaking, telemarketing, media coverage (press releases, articles, radio coverage) and strategic alliances.

During her entire career, she was very involved in clubs and organizations, constantly networking and speaking. When she first moved to Miami over 45 years ago, she didn't know a soul. She read the newspapers to find out what clubs were meeting. She would attend with a specific goal: to meet five new people at each event, and remember the ones that she met the previous month. That's what she did with every free night. The first year in Miami, she met 1200 people. She found ways to stay in touch with them and consequently became very well known in the city.

> She had a specific goal to meet five new people at each event. Within one year, she met 1200 people.

Gayle has always been the telemarketing queen, very comfortable on the phone. She sold her schools and her speaking abilities through the telephone, and has learned to uncover a lot of information through questions. She picked up those phone skills when she was eight years old. Her father was a pharmacist, and she had to be able to answer the telephone at her house properly, and then call in the drug orders. It was a bit of a struggle to even pronounce those complicated medical and pharmaceutical words, but it gave her a strong foundation in phone relations. Selling by phone has since become more challenging than ever. These days, people don't answer their own phones, they transfer calls into voice mail, and e-mail has taken over.

During her speaking and training career, she worked hard to land reputable media coverage. For instance, she graced the cover of *USA Today* after responding to a survey of "road warriors." Out of all the respondents, she was the only one who loved to travel and enjoyed being on the road for business. She also appeared as a guest on the *Larry King Show*. Gayle knew Larry because he was the emcee for the Ms. Florida pageant for seven years – which was organized by Gayle's company.

Her top marketing tools were sending press releases and writing articles. When she received an award or some recognition, she would send out press releases. Her philosophy was that if 50 press releases were sent, 48 would probably be trashed but two would be printed somewhere. Her strategy was so successful that people would call up asking, "Who do you use to do your PR?" It was just Gayle and her assistant. When she was on the road so much, they put her speaking dates on a postcard and sent them out. For example, if she was going to do eight or 10 speaking engagements in a particular state, they would send mail to the associations and the meeting planners in that state, listing the dates she was going to be there and the dates in between that she would be available. That way, it wouldn't cost them as much to bring her in.

She has done over 500 radio talk shows. It's a very easy marketing tool because you can do a talk show from anywhere – you don't have to be physically in the studio. She did them at all hours ... even 3 a.m ... as well as anytime she could during the day ... sometimes in her pajamas ... sometimes in a phone booth ... in an airport ... in a hotel lobby ... or between speaking engagements. In the early 90s, when her book *Winning Ways: How to Get to the Top and Stay There* came out, she did 200 to 250 radio shows in one year. One time, she went to a speaking engagement in Kansas City, called some independent bookstores and asked them if they would feature her book – which they did, so she sent them copies. Then she called three radio talk shows and one local television talk show and asked if they would like to have her on as their guest on that particular day and they said yes. So she did three radio shows and one television talk show, then steered the people in Kansas City to the independent bookstores. The books sold out. Then she went back to the convention center in Kansas City and did her speech, which was on marketing. She had a perfect example of how to market and be successful at it.

A few years ago, she realized that the business environment has changed and she needed to change as well, or else it could be devastating. She started to form alliances. In 2001, she put together a "Who's Who" list and contacted 12 people. She felt they would complement each other and everyone could make more money. She managed to contact nine of them and five or six projects came through. They agreed to write together, collaborate on consulting gigs and refer customers to each other. One person offered his entire client list. In that year alone she tripled her business.

Choose your niche wisely

When Gayle started speaking over 20 years ago, her primary industry was healthcare. Even though she wasn't a healthcare professional, there were many people in that industry who hired her. She also worked in the utility sector and with many different associations. Now, with the changes in those industries (laws, regulations, etc.), her focus has changed as well. She has emerged as a specialist in customer service. In fact, she recently appeared on ABC as a customer service expert. She was also brought over to Melbourne, Australia, as the keynote speaker for the Australian Customer Service Summit.

A well-known brand is specific to the industry and audience that it serves. In other words, there are people in every industry – technology, science, medicine, education, management, small businesses, government, etc. – who are very highly respected and branded personally; yet outside of that industry, no one knows them. It happens that you are a brand and yet you are not a brand, depending on your chosen area – your niche. Once you have chosen the niche, Gayle recommends looking at what is really needed. In other words, what can you offer that isn't there yet? What are the problems in that niche and how can you make them easier? Then, take that insight and shape it so people buy and use your product of service. Offer it in a way that is marketable.

> A well-known brand is relative to the industry and audience that it serves.

Embark on new ventures

Now she is embarking on a new phase of her career, retooling her business so she can spend more time at home with her husband. A few years ago, her husband got sick and she didn't want to travel like she had been. She covered about a quarter of a million miles a year. She is spending 80 percent of her time building a coaching and education business using the Internet. At the moment, she is transferring 12 courses into an online format for use by various companies. That includes rewriting all the course materials, adding audio and creating visuals suitable for online use. Students will be able to watch and listen, and when they believe they have mastered the material, they can take an exam.

The remaining part of her time will be spent on women's entrepreneurial retreats in Miami Beach. The program will combine fitness and business advice for women between 45 and 65 who want to go into business for themselves. Since she is an older woman, she is repositioning herself in that market and will show those women that you are never too old to do something, whatever it is. She believes that the fitness aspects are particularly important. Gayle sets the example. "I used to be the youngest at everything; now I'm the oldest, but I feel the youngest," she says. "I think my strength will be in showing women how to be independent after 50. There are many over-50 women who are going through big life changes. They have lost spouses, either through divorce or death, and they are at a loss. There is a big need."

Her website features a picture of Gayle in her workout outfit, in front of a yacht, jumping in the air, with a briefcase in one hand, which has "Wiz of Biz" on it, and with money in the other hand. She says, "I want to show a successful woman who has energy, is confident and is okay on her own making money."

Learn new things

Gayle is always learning and discovering. Every evening, she writes down the answers to two questions:

1. What is one positive thing that happened today?

2. What did I learn today?

"I'm always excited about new things. I think there is so much I need to learn, and I think that is wonderful," she says.

Friends that have known Gayle from her roots say that she never gives up. She just keep going and going and going. Some of her former school friends have retired. They have no desire to work anymore. They would never do the things she does, or go the places she goes, whereas she has gone all over the world by herself. She will always be in business and will always be doing things because that's just who she is.

Gayle loves the feeling of accomplishment, the feeling she is contributing to others, the feeling that she's providing a service that is needed and people benefit from. It's important to her that when people finish listening to her, they learned something. When she was president of an association, she brought in new methodologies, new revenue streams, and new policies that made a difference. She feels she has left a mark.

Eight insights from Gayle Carson on Making Things Happen

1. Life isn't fair, but you have to survive anyway so always be prepared for the worst and enjoy the best.

2. Always treat people better than you want to be treated.

3. Keep your ethics and values intact. Live your life according to your values – no one else's. Don't ever compromise your ethics.

4. Set a goal, get focused and do your homework. Hard work never hurt anyone, so go at it.

5. Wake up every day with a smile, and if you don't, find out why.

6. Live a balanced life, whatever that means to you.

7. Don't be afraid to dream and take risks. Think about how you want to be remembered.

8. Follow you own path. Share your passion.

Gayle Carson's Viewpoints

Make people pay attention to your business

There are many ways to generate useful publicity for your business: take a survey, create a contest, or proclaim a "this is my business" day. Remember, your goal is to get people talking about you. The potential benefits are enormous – even if people don't do business with you, they probably know somebody who will.

Create a winning image

Image is what people think of you the minute they see you – your office, store, stationery, business card, the way you answer the telephone, how you treat your customer and even your e-mails. That impression is developed in the first 10 to 30 seconds, and you can spend the rest of your business relationship trying to change it. You need to decide what you want that image to be.

Speaking in public – with confidence – as a way to get noticed and stay noticed

One of the most important skills you will ever need is the ability to stand in front of a group and do a talk. You may be heading a committee, making a sales presentation, running for a volunteer position or doing a sound bite on television – people who speak effectively and can communicate their message have an advantage. If there was ever one course I would make sure every man, woman and child took, it would be a course in public speaking. Go to Toastmasters or join a networking group where you have to stand up and introduce yourself and tell what you do. The confidence that you can get up and speak puts you one step ahead of a lot of other people. Start practicing now.

Networking

Networking goes far beyond just shaking hands and trading business cards. Networking means making people understand exactly what you do, how you do it and why you do it. It also means showing how that translates into benefits for their clients, people they know who could use your products or services, and why you should be considered a leader in your field. There is no better way to get business from a person than to give them business. An expert networker puts people together and helps them make deals – without any expectation of returns.

Growing your business

In preparing for growth, the most important thing is being able to replicate yourself. As a small business owner you can duplicate the system you use, have other people open a business under your name or have additional locations that other people can run. At one time, I had seven different offices with various managers, and they all ran pretty smoothly. Yes, I had to make sure everything was on target, but my employees all did a fantastic job and believed in what we did as much as I did.

Staying motivated

Motivation is a positive energy that we can generate and harness. I stay motivated by coping with stress effectively. Stress comes from high demand and low control. My coping mechanisms are exercise, pets and water. For you they might be music, art, walks or nature. Whatever your method, find ways to cope.

Consider the people and things you surround yourself with

Five minutes of negative thinking can take up to 24 hours to recover from. Some of us live or work with negative people. You may need to make changes. Take charge, set up your parameters, do what you say is important. Remember – no one can change anyone else. It is up to you to make your life the way you want it.

Maintaining good health

To have stamina, it is important to stay in shape and feel good. Fitness divides into a couple of categories. The first one is what you eat. It is not up to me to dictate your diet plan, but you need to understand your body and how certain foods affect you. The second part is exercise, and that is something I am vehement about. Whether it is walking, swimming, weight training or yoga, exercise is mandatory for circulation, energy and general good health. Thirty minutes a day can do it for you – everyone should be able to find that amount of time. The third part is keeping in touch with your physician for annual checkups. Listen to what your doctor (and your body) says. Prevention is the best method of staying well.[1]

Simon Says:

Go to www.gaylecarson.com and sign up for Gayle's e-mail newsletter under E-Zine. You will receive a weekly *Wiz of Biz Tip* to help you run your life in a more productive and happy way. It will bring you new energy to help you "stay at the top."

BRIAN TRACY
on
Pushing to the Front

There are more than 10,000 professional and non-professional speakers competing in the U.S. market today. Brian Tracy has pushed forward to become one of the world's leading authorities on personal and business effectiveness. His seminars and publications on sales, leadership, managerial effectiveness and business strategy are loaded with proven strategies that people can quickly apply to get better results. He has written 26 books, produced more than 300 audio and video learning programs, and has given presentations in 24 countries. Each year, approximately 250,000 people benefit from attending his seminars across the globe.

Brian describes success through the analogy of a marathon. Those who are ahead of the field take small and steady steps and gradually distance themselves from their competitors. They steadily push toward the front. This chapter profiles how Brian developed his brand, and what steps he took to move ahead in today's business race.

Learn what works

Brian Tracy considers himself a *professional* speaker rather than a *motivational* speaker. His key focus, the central component of his brand identity or brand statement, is to give people practical tools and ideas through speaking, writing and learning programs that can be put into practice. He speaks on several different subjects – strategy, sales, business development, management, leadership, creative thinking, personal performance and goal setting – in a very motivational way, but it's *practical* material. It revolves around solid ideas that people can apply to get better results.

Brian grew up in Vancouver, Canada, and came from a poor background with few advantages. During his teen years, he worked at various laboring jobs; in the winter he worked in hotels and restaurants, washing pots and pans, and in the summer he worked on ranches and farms. He also worked on a Norwegian freighter in the North Atlantic as a galley boy, in construction as a laborer and in factories putting nuts on bolts, hour after hour.

At age 20, Brian was ready for a change in his life, willing to step out and take risks. Brian and his two best friends, Geoff and Bob, had a big dream. They wanted to travel the world. With only $300 in their pockets, they set out on a long journey. The three young men crossed North America from west to east, then sailed across the Atlantic Ocean, traveled the length of Europe from London to Gibraltar, and then crossed Africa from Morocco to South Africa. It was a distance of more than 17,000 miles, through dozens of countries. Those 12 months were the most impressionable time in Brian's life. He learned one lesson that never left him: To achieve a big goal, the most important step is the first one. All the rest follow from that.[1]

Throughout his travels, he read continually. His thirst for knowledge helped shape his career and philosophy on life. Eventually, he learned that if you do the right things in the right way consistently, you can get extraordinary results in much less time. Brian has spent his whole life looking for the cause-and-effect relationships between doing certain things and getting certain results. It's very much like a recipe in the kitchen. If you have a good recipe and you practice it often, you will prepare a good dish. You can have all the best ingredients – which is to say you can have a great mind, live in a great society, have a great education, discover great opportunities, all of these things – but if you don't have the recipes, these things won't do you any good. However, with the right recipes, an average person with average opportunities can do extraordinary things. Brian's whole life and purpose has been focused on finding these recipes.

> With the right recipes, you can do anything you set out to do.

Twenty years ago, Brian asked himself, "Why is it that some people are more successful than others?" He made it his goal to find out what makes successful people stand apart, whether in sales, management, leadership or any field. He identified those reasons, almost like scientifically trying to find the cause or cure of a disease, and then duplicated the process. For example, when Brian got into sales, he found that top sales people simply sold professionally. Consequently, he learned how to sell professionally. When he got into sales management, he discovered that top managers recruited, trained and managed better. So, he learned how to recruit, train and manage better. When he got into real estate development, he read 20 books on the subject and then was able to buy property and develop it. When he got into training, advertising, or any other field, he simply learned how. "This is really exciting to me; with the right recipes, you can do anything you set out to do."

True motivation

Brian is a self-taught man, committed to learning something new each day. After making the jump from sales to sales management, Brian began attending public seminars, but he wasn't impressed. He found most of them to be of poor quality, and he was inspired do better than the speakers he heard. He thought, "I'm going to give a seminar. I'm going to take all the ideas that I've learned and put them together in a system. I have learned that any system is better than no system. Everything has a beginning, middle and end. It has a series of practical things that you do and they are all hooked together. Again, it comes back to a recipe. Any recipe is better than no recipe."

Brian put his "system" together by pulling information from his comprehensive collection of books and articles: nearly 10,000 books and thousands of articles. He started his career by targeting personal transformation and performance improvement. Today, the purpose of his work is to help people achieve their goals faster than they could without his help.

Brian's work is marked by high content and high energy. His passion is like the powder in a cartridge, and the hard-hitting content is the bullet. The passion is a driving force, providing the "hitting power."

Whether speaking to a crowd of 20,000 or to a couple of individuals, Brian maintains a single focus – to help people get vastly more out of themselves, and to give them practical tools or techniques to do it. Brian makes a clear distinction between two types of motivation: there's a false motivation and true one. False motivation is like throwing gasoline on a fire. It has a big puff and then, it's gone. True motivation, on the other hand, is more like throwing a log on a fire. It burns and burns and burns for a long time. He emphasizes true motivation ... that is, practical, actionable ideas.

> Any system is better than no system.

Brian doesn't rely too much on emotions, compared to other speakers in his field. For example, the big difference between Tony Robbins and Brian is that Tony is focused on emotion. While he tries to get to the brain from the heart, Brian goes to the heart from the brain.

His approach has been particularly well received in Europe. In 2001, Brian won the "Success Trainer of the Year" award in Germany. The reason for his speaking success in Europe is that Europeans, and Germans in particular, are pragmatic. They want practical concepts. This is exactly what he provides, along with an entertaining element to make it enjoyable. He has always believed that education does not have to be painful. You can learn great ideas in an entertaining way.

Let your brand emerge

Brian's brand has been a process of evolution through hard work. For example, he reads an average of three hours a day, consuming at least two books, four newspapers and about 30 magazines each week. He also listens to a number of audio programs and attends educational seminars. He stays very much on the front edge of his field and continually learns new material. In fact, every time he speaks on a particular topic, the presentation has evolved and matured.

An area of excellence tends to appear as you move forward. Brian didn't start out with a brand identity. He ended up with a one. He calls this evolutionary process his "bottom up" strategy. It's like backing into something, getting out of the car to see what you ran over, and it turns out to be your brand. A brand tends to emerge. A mission tends to emerge. Soon you find that the people who hire you, buy your materials or compliment you are all saying the same things. For Brian, it was "great ideas"... "practical" ... "easy to digest."

Deliver excellence

Like a doctor who specializes in one area of medicine, a lawyer who specializes in one type of client or a writer who specializes in one genre, Brian advises professionals in service businesses to develop excellence and focus their energy in one area. Identify something you can do, and then do it better than anyone else. Instead of spreading your energy over a wide area, focus in on two or three things you can do really, really well. Identify a particular customer who would benefit from exceptional service in that area. Focus on becoming very, very good at that – *absolutely excellent*. And then, constantly look for ways to do it better.

Brian recommends people to ask themselves three basic questions:

1. *If you were financially independent, what would you choose to do in terms of your work?*
   The answer to this question is what gives you the greatest satisfaction and self-esteem. That is the thing that you can do the best. It gives you the most energy and makes you happiest.

2. *If you could only do one thing at work, what would you choose to do all day long?*
   This question separates your brand from everything else you do.

3. *How do you organize your life in such a way so that you are doing that all day long, and doing it really well?*

When you answer these questions, you'll tap into a new level of clarity about your life. Your chances for long-term satisfaction and success are measurably higher when you identify your strengths and reorient your business around them.

Brian strives to represent this philosophy in his own life. Given the chance, he would speak to an audience all day long. He's energized and excited by the opportunity to speak to people, give advice and help change their attitudes about themselves and their futures. He loves to help them set goals and develop a clear vision for where they want to go; change their way of thinking so they're solution-oriented instead of problem-oriented; let go of the past; exemplify excellence and focus on becoming better and better at the most important things they do. If he can encourage someone to try something new or grow in a different direction, it's a great day. These are the things that really matter to him. As he says, "If you have them, you

> Focus on becoming very, very good – absolutely excellent – at something.

have everything. If you don't, you got nothing." He adds, "If I could do it all day long, I would do keynotes and seminars for interested, curious and positive audiences. I'm doing what I enjoy and I get better and better at it. I take coaching in it all the time. I study the craft of speaking all the time. I'm constantly working at becoming better both in delivery and in high content."

Develop winning habits

In his new book, *Million Dollar Habit*, Brian explores the notion that people are *where* they are and *what* they are because of their habits. Most of the things that people do are automatic. Good habits in each area of your life ensure positive, productive experiences. For example, regarding money Brian said, "People with good financial habits, even if they only earn an average living, will become financially independent. People without good habits will be broke, even if they make a lot of money."

Through his research and work, Brian has found that people are successful because they identify a habit that they need to cultivate, and then they practice it until it becomes second nature. It becomes an automatic behavior. "Over time, if you've developed a habit for speed, dependability, quality work, punctuality and being prepared ... Surprise! Surprise! ... You'll be promoted faster, paid more money, see more doors open up for you, attract better people into your life, and so on."

After many years of studying this concept and tracking it in his work, Brian has identified approximately 120 habits that successful people develop. That may seem like a lot, but they are small things ... like being punctual, planning your day in advance and wearing your seatbelt. Despite their small significance in the larger scope of your life, the cumulative effect is quite extraordinary. The key to remember is: all habits are learnable.

Listen to the market

Perception is critical in personal brand management. It is not who *you* think you are. It's about who *other people* think you are.

Brian gets e-mails all the time from people saying, "I'm having problems with my career." His response is quite simple: "Well, you're going to have to change your career. There's nobody that needs that kind of work today because that's gone." And they say, "But I can't seem to get a job doing what I want to do." The secret is, "You have to do what your *customer* wants. You have to do what your *market* wants. You have to focus on a niche for which there is a distinctive and identifiable market. There's no point in specializing, differentiating, segmenting, concentrating and then marketing something that people don't want."

> You have to do what your customer wants. You have to do what your market wants.

Identifying the customer and understanding what they value is essential. It goes back to the basic questions from business guru Peter Drucker:

- Who is my customer?

- What does my customer consider value?

- What is it that I do especially well for my customer that my customer considers valuable?

Brian has let his brand develop in response to his market. Though it may not be tangible, his focus on his audience, reader or listener is part of his brand. What really matters is how others perceive Brian Tracy, and what they say or think about him.

To get different results you've got to do things differently

Brian enjoys telling stories about personal transformation. "A guy wrote to me. He was in sales and was just about to quit. He lived in Phoenix and was on his way to an appointment with a customer in Palm Springs, which is about a three-hour drive. He got a set of my audio programs and began listening. As he drove across the desert, he got so caught up in the program that he kept driving. He drove all the way to San Francisco listening to the program, turned around and drove all the way back to Palm Springs. He learned why it is that people act the way they do, why they are where they are in life, the specific things that can be done to get a different result ... and that when people do those things, they get a different result. When he called on his customer, he made the biggest sale of his life and it changed his whole career. He said he was a completely different person from then on.

> To achieve something you've never achieved before, you must do something you've never done before.

"The wonderful thing about this story – and I've heard many wonderful stories from people who have driven across the country listening to my materials – is he got it, and he used it to get a different result."

There are no shortcuts around hard work

Brian does not consider himself a genius, but his ability to synthesize information – to take information from various sources and apply them to new courses, books or talks – is remarkable. What really sets him apart is his work ethic. Brian simply works *hard*.

"It's like running a race," he said. "If you run really hard, you slowly create a distance between you and the other runners and you eventually widen that distance and get further and further ahead. Eventually, you're so far ahead that people wonder how you got there. Well, it's no miracle. I just worked hard." Too often, people are always looking for shortcuts ... but there are no shortcuts around hard work. "Some people think, 'Well no, it's the brand ... you just have to get a brand.' However, your brand has to be a true brand. It has to be a brand that has a solid, concrete foundation underneath it. It's got to be built on something. Some people have said, 'I want to be the next Brian Tracy.' My friend, who runs my office, says 'Well, you'll never make it.' And they wonder, 'How can you say that?' She says to them, 'Because you're not willing to work as hard as Brian is.'"

> The reason some people are successful is because they work harder than others.

Although Brian works hard, he values his time off. He takes off 150 days each year, including three weeks around Christmas. But between vacations, he *really* works. He works 10-12 hour days, sometimes seven days a week. The vacations are crucial to maintaining his work regimen. He understands work-life balance. "Taking time off is terribly important when I'm doing brain work. Otherwise, my mind will burn out. I'll become tired."

Commit to mastery

Mastery is one of Brian's most popular subjects. Mastery means you have reached the point where you are really good at what you're doing and you're recognized as really good. Achieving mastery is a difficult challenge, especially in marketing and branding. According to his research, it takes five to seven years to achieve mastery at something. Very few people ever achieve mastery in less than seven years. Some people never achieve it at all because they don't realize it takes a lot of hard work. They end up frustrated because they're not successful, but they don't work really, really hard.

Sometimes he jokes with his audiences and says, "You know it takes five to seven years to get in the top 10 percent in the field of selling. Once you get into that area, you'll earn $100,000, $200,000 ... even $300,000 a year. You'll have one of the best incomes and you'll probably never go back, but it takes five to seven years. A lot of people complain, 'That's an awfully long time to get to the top of your field.' But here's my observation ... the time is going to pass *anyway*, so it's only a matter of what are you going to do with that time? You don't want to turn back five or seven years from now and say, 'Oh my! If I had started earlier, I'd be at the top of my field today.' If you are patient, you say to yourself, 'Okay, it's going to take five to seven years to achieve mastery. So, I'm going to work very, very hard for five to seven years until I get there." If you're willing to do that, you can be assured that when the five to seven years has passed, you'll be there."

Keep moving forward

Brian uses his numerous speaking events to market himself and his learning programs. He gives around 100 presentations each year, including 20-25 overseas. Brian facilitates both public and private seminars. He speaks at organizational meetings and conventions. He works with corporations. He does strategic planning sessions for management groups and coaches at the executive level.

Books are another key component of his marketing strategy. He constantly writes. At the time of this interview, Brian had published five books in the previous year and had four books under contract for the coming year. Every time a book comes out, it goes into all of the bookstores. His public relations firm makes sure he gets about 100-150 radio and television interviews on each book. They also get his books excerpted in dozens of magazines and newspapers. Some of the books sell a lot, others don't.

The talks and the books are working well for him, but he's quick to point out that there's never one thing that accounts for success. It's many different things. He has to hustle all of the time, keep working continuously. It's a constant process of moving forward, developing new talks, reading new material and always developing new content.

Try new things

Brian is committed to staying open to new possibilities, new ideas, new avenues. His view of the universe is that *the more you give of yourself without expectation of return, the more things will come back to you in the most unexpected ways*. He will often invest numerous hours to explore possibilities or to help other people push something forward – and many of them don't pay off. In business, he finds that about nine out of 10 things don't work out. In fact, if one out of 10 works out, he's happy. The key is to try many things.

Learning is another key component of his strategy for success. Every time he learns something new, his endorphins trigger a feeling of happiness. Brian views retirement as a 20th century concept that goes back to the agricultural and industrial age, when people would work until their bodies were no longer capable. But it's different for people who work with their minds. They don't retire.

> The more you give of yourself without expectation, the more things will come back to you in the most unexpected ways.

As Brian told his 65-year-old friend, "You know, you're at the top of your game today. You're the best you've ever been." His friend responded, "You're right. I am. I've never been sharper, never been brighter, and never been more experienced."

He recites an article about the direct relationship between mental activity and long life, and the correlation with Alzheimer's disease or other impairments. The more mentally active people are, the brighter they are, the more energy they have and the longer they live.

Brian enjoys what he does. He loves his work. That's why he'll probably never retire.

Six Insights from Brian Tracy on Pushing to the Front

1. Find something you can do better than anybody else. Then become really, really good at that.
2. Listen carefully to market and the clients. Know what they value, what they need, what they want. Then offer a solution.
3. Develop winning habits ... day by day.
4. Work hard and smart. Hard work combined with the right recipes or system will get you to the top.
5. Commit to achieving mastery. It easily takes an average of five to seven years to become excellent at something.
6. Continue to try new things. Make use of the Law of Averages. The more you try, the more often you will succeed.

Brian Tracy's Viewpoints

On Building Confidence

Confidence is a habit that can be developed by acting as if you already had the confidence you desire to have.

On Overcoming Obstacles

For every person who stops succeeding because of a difficulty, there are thousands who have had it a lot worse and succeeded anyway. So can you.

You have within you, right now, deep reserves of potential and ability that, properly harnessed and channeled, will enable you to accomplish extraordinary things with you life. The only real limits on what you can do, have, or be, are self-imposed. They do not exist outside of you.

On the Law of Attraction

You become what you think about most of the time. If you admire successful people, you create a positive force field of attraction that pulls you to become more and more like the kinds of people that you admire.

Whatever you concentrate on grows. Life is the study of attention. Where your attention goes, your heart goes. Your ability to divert your attention from activities of lower value to activities of higher value is central to everything you accomplish in life.

On Winning

The act of taking the first step is what separates the winners from the losers. The ability to discipline yourself to delay gratification in the short term in order to enjoy greater rewards in the long term is the indispensable prerequisite for success.

On Sales

Selling has often been called a *transfer of enthusiasm*. The level of belief in the value of a product or service is directly related to the ability to convince other people that it is good for them.

The two major enemies in sales are the fear of failure or loss, and the fear of criticism or rejection.

On Goals

Every single life becomes great when the individual sets upon a goal or goals which they really believe in, which they can really commit themselves to, which they can put their whole heart and soul into.

The key to success is to set one big, challenging goal and then pay any price, overcome any obstacle, and persist through any difficulty until you finally achieve it.

On Time Management

There will never be enough time to do everything you have to do.

On Your Most Precious Resource

Your ability to think is your most precious resource. Your ability to choose your own thoughts and reactions is the one thing over which you have complete control.[2]

Simon Says:

Listen to Brian Tracy's audio program *Advanced Selling Techniques*. It is available at www.briantracy.com.

Brian's approach to selling is practical and pragmatic. His six-CD audio program, convenient for listening in the car, covers all aspects of selling. He provides tools to get more appointments, uncover the real need, increase sales effectiveness, develop credibility and much more.

JIM KOUZES
on
Becoming a Leader

Jim Kouzes, a renowned leader in leadership development, is the co-author of the award-winning book, The Leadership Challenge. *Now in its third edition, the book is a* Business Week *bestseller with over one million copies sold in 14 languages. Jim is also an executive fellow at the Center for Innovation and Entrepreneurship at the Leavey School of Business, Santa Clara University.* The Wall Street Journal *has cited Jim as one of the 12 most requested "non-university executive-education providers" to U. S. companies. A popular speaker, Jim shares lessons about leadership that have arisen from over 20 years of original research.*

What do leadership and personal branding have in common? Based on Jim Kouzes' own experience and research, this chapter offers practical answers.

Co-branding as collaboration

For Jim Kouzes, a brand is a total *experience*. "It's not something that you stick on the outside of a package," he says. "It's something that comes from the inside. To understand your brand you have to understand your own life experiences and the meaning of those experiences."

His book *The Leadership Challenge* was shaped by his life experiences, and is the result of many collaborations. The most important of those partnerships is the one with Barry Posner, Dean of the Leavey School of Business at Santa Clara University. Barry is his co-author, colleague and best friend. They've been writing and working together since 1981 – more than 20 years. While they certainly have their individual identities, their brand is a collaborative creation.

"There's not one shred of evidence that leadership – or that achieving anything great – is a solo act," says Jim. "I once asked Don Bennett, the first amputee to climb Mt. Rainier, to tell me the most important lesson he learned in making that famous climb. Without hesitation, he said, 'You can't do it alone.' That phrase has stuck with me for two decades. Today, I'm convinced of it more than ever. You can't do it alone. I certainly know that from my own experience. Barry and I have found from our research involving thousands of leaders that those who score higher on collaboration are more effective in meeting the demands of their jobs. I'd be a hypocrite if I didn't live that value in my own life."

That collaborative spirit is a part of every thing Jim does. Before publishing anything that will have both their names on it, Barry and Jim discuss everything they write. They split all the royalties 50/50. Jim says with sincerity, "There's no such thing as saying, 'I'm going to write 80% of this so I'm going to get 80% of the royalties.' Partnerships fall apart when that happens. For us, it's always been 50/50. We have always known in our hearts that we couldn't do this without the other person. Developing our brand and being successful in the marketplace has been a collaborative effort."

At the same time, while they split the work and the rewards 50/50, their work has to be of one voice. It has to be in harmony. If they're out of tune or out of synch with each other, they can't create a compelling product. If someone could say, "Oh, Jim wrote that part, and Barry wrote that other part," they wouldn't have a unified brand. Collaboration has to yield a unified experience to result in a successful brand. To ensure that their writing speaks with one voice, there's a lot of back-and-forth and give-and-take. The process may take longer, but the result is something that neither could have produced by acting alone. "That doesn't mean that we sit side-by-side and write each sentence together," Jim notes, "nor does it mean that we've submerged our individuality. We just learned how to build on each other's strengths and use our talents to better effect through collaboration."

Jim's affinity for leadership goes back a long way

Jim grew up in the suburbs of Washington, D.C. Because of his proximity to the nation's capital, he was immersed in American politics and the making of world history. From the time he was a sophomore in high school, he shared his home with many foreign students from the Middle East, South America, Europe, Asia and Africa. His mother continued this tradition after his father passed away in 1977, and he and his family are very proud of the fact that over 100 young men and women have called their house "home." This has blessed him with the opportunity to live, work and play with people of many different backgrounds, religions, nationalities and belief systems. This experience is reflected in his brand.

Growing up in the nation's capital also afforded him some other wonderful opportunities. January 20, 1961, for example, was a life-changing day. That was the date of John F. Kennedy's inauguration, and Jim was one of a dozen Eagle Scouts selected to serve in John F. Kennedy's Honor Guard at the presidential inauguration. That day is burned in his memory, and he points to it as one of those seminal moments when he knew he had found his calling to be of service. Inspired by Kennedy and other leaders of the 1960s, Jim joined the Peace Corps after college and served as a volunteer from 1967 through 1969.

The Peace Corps introduced Jim to the realities of living in another culture and speaking another language. "A friend once told me," Jim says, "that to speak another language fluently is to have another soul. I came away from the Peace Corps

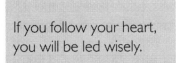

If you follow your heart, you will be led wisely.

with a profound understanding and awareness that we're all connected. We can be of one soul, but we have to listen with our eyes and our hearts." He adds, "The profound possibility also exists that we can realize a dream of peace and freedom. I learned, however, that achieving peace and freedom is a struggle. We all have to work very hard at it."

The Peace Corps also introduced Jim to social psychology and applied behavioral sciences, the disciplines that underlie leadership and organizational behavior. "Many people think leadership is firmly grounded in individual psychology. While Freud and Jung have certainly influenced the field, the more significant contributions have come from social psychology," Jim notes. During his Peace Corps training and immediately afterwards, Jim had the chance to study with some of the most notable experts in the field.

Putting leadership to the test

Jim became active in the Organizational Development (OD) Network in 1975, and he chaired the 1980 national conference in San Francisco. As chairperson, he wanted to do something different. Being a strong believer in collaboration, he decided to put his values to the test.

He and his committee members opened up the planning

process to everyone who wanted to be involved. They let every member of the OD Network in the Bay Area know that if they wanted to be involved in the planning of this conference they were welcome to contribute in whatever way fit their own timeframe, availability, talents and aspirations allowed. Ultimately, over 300 people came together to plan and execute the conference. It was the largest conference of the OD Network to date and it brought in significant revenue. That event taught him an important lesson: Collaboration is successful if (1) you believe in it, and (2) you use a process that can involve people in a meaningful way. He considers the event to be one of his best personal leadership experiences. It was a turning point in his life.

One of the presenters at the conference was André Delbecq. André later became the dean of the Leavey School of Business at Santa Clara University, and he asked Jim if he would consider taking a job there. In 1981, Jim became director of the Executive Development Center at Santa Clara University. That job connected him to Barry Posner. They shared an affinity for the same kinds of issues and they were both attracted to the subject of leadership, so they decided to team up. Their joint work began as an intensive research project on leadership, and the academic setting helped to shape another characteristic of their brand – their emphasis on rigorous research.

Jim and Barry were troubled by some of their research into leadership and corporate culture because they found assertions that leadership only existed in excellent companies. They had both observed that there are good leaders in bad companies and bad leaders in good companies. "Leadership is not the private reserve of a few charismatic men and women who happened to join a few organizations," Jim points out. "First of all, that's a demographic impossibility. Secondly, to say that leadership is confined to a very few excellent companies is a denial of all the great leadership that exists outside of them."

Jim and Barry looked around and noted that there are

leaders in all countries, all organizations, all political systems and all religions. "There are youth leaders, senior leaders, team leaders, leaders who get paid and leaders who volunteer. Leadership knows no racial or religious bounds, no ethnic or cultural borders. The idea of learning about leadership by studying only a few exceptional corporate leaders was wrongheaded," says Jim. He and Barry wanted to know *the common and transferable leadership practices of many different leaders from varied backgrounds*. They've taken a more universal approach to leadership, not one that's focused on corporations or on leaders at the very top of the hierarchy. They developed a strong belief – which is backed by research – that leadership is everyone's business.

> "What are the common leadership practices of many different leaders from varied backgrounds?" That question became the foundation of the book *The Leadership Challenge*.

Barry and Jim set out to create a valid and reliable model that was simple, useable and practical. They decided to study leadership using a "Personal Best Leadership Experiences" methodology. They asked people to tell a story about a time when they did their best as leaders. They figured that if they looked at enough stories, they would find common themes across those stories, and then they might be able to make some generalizations about leadership. From there they could test the hypothesis in a variety of settings and see if they held up empirically. The outcome was *The Leadership Challenge*.

Brand power comes from substance

While Jim and Barry had strong affiliations with Santa Clara University, they wanted to reach beyond academia and write in a style that would address a broader audience. Most students of the executive program at the business school were in business settings. They wanted a book that was effortless to read and geared toward the everyday leader and manager.

They began with the assumption, based on their research, that "leadership is everyone's business," and approached their writing from that perspective.

Barry and Jim strongly believed in their work. They were in love with the subject matter and hoped people would read their message. They had no idea that the book would sell as well as it did, but they did have an aspiration early on that when people thought about leadership, one of the three books that would come to mind would be *The Leadership Challenge*. While this was their aspiration, it was never about the money. It was their passion that drove them. The book was a vehicle for the expression of their passion and research.

It was at least fifteen years after the book was published that they started to talk about their work as a brand. In the latter part of the 1990s, in preparation for the third edition of *The Leadership Challenge*, their publisher commissioned a study to find out why people bought their book, why people bought business books in general, and what readers wanted from the book. The data helped them define what it was about Barry Posner and Jim Kouzes and their work that was compelling for the readers. Building a brand was not something they set out to create. They had established a brand without really knowing it. They worked because they loved their work, but over time, as people experienced them and their work, a brand emerged.

The experience creates the brand.

Jim is certain that if somebody starts out wanting to become a brand, it's less likely to happen than if they just be who they are. It's all about integrity; the opposite of integrity is hypocrisy. "You can't create something that you're not. You're just acting; just playing a part. Without substance, you won't survive very

A genuine brand has to be rooted in a passion or cause or something of deep commitment.

long as a brand because it becomes about ego, about me, wonderful me. A genuine brand has to be rooted in a passion, a cause or a deep commitment. Being on the cover of *Fortune* magazine does not make a person a brand. That kind of iconography is not what branding is. You've got to start out with a passion for something. That passion becomes magnetic to people. People are drawn to it. There's a point at which you have to say, 'That's our original work, not somebody else's.' When you are original and you have your own unique voice, the audience doesn't even have to see you to know who is behind the work. When someone says Madonna or The Beatles or Bob Dylan or Steven Spielberg or Daffy Duck, you probably get images in your mind. You would be able to identify these characters without prompting."

At the Cinequest Film Festival in San Jose, California, Jim listened to a filmmaker comment on his recently released film. After being rejected by traditional Hollywood financing agencies, he financed his film through friends and family. In response to an audience question about why he did it, the director said, "This film had to be made." People who are successful and established in a field share this trait of zeal and obsession. They *have* to do it. That's what it means to be driven. They are going after their passion. It's in their soul. It's who they are. It's not just turning out books or doing work to make a buck. It's about long-term sustainability. You have to love what you're doing. It has to be what gets you up in the morning.

To Jim, Peter Drucker is an excellent example of this point. How much time has Peter Drucker ever spent asking himself about his brand? Probably not much. Yet he's still the best-known writer and management consultant in the industry. Why is that? Peter just does what is important to him ... what's in

> You have to love what you're doing. It has to be what gets you up in the morning.

his heart ... and people respond.

Whenever Jim works on a project, he asks himself a lot of questions about why he's doing it: "What's my aspiration? What's my passion? What drives me? What's important to me?" He adds, "If I'm not successful in selling a particular book, I don't feel badly because I'm doing what I love to do. Otherwise, if I am successful, I consider myself to be blessed. I also know that our success is a function of many things, including a lot of hard work and some good luck."

Liberate the leader in everyone

When Jim conducted the first residential workshop using their new research on leadership, one of his co-trainers was Ann Bowers, who at the time was vice president of human resources at Apple Computer. Before they started the workshop, Ann said to him, "Jim, you write about vision. You advise leaders to have a vision. What's *your* vision?" Jim responded without hesitation, "To liberate the leader in everyone."

> Leaders don't get appointed. It's earned through behavior. You only become a leader when other people want to follow you.

Jim goes on to explain that leadership isn't about a title or position. "Just because you have the title of president doesn't make you a leader. Leaders don't get appointed. It's earned through their behavior. Leadership is defined more by someone's constituents than by that person. People only become leaders when other people want to follow them."

Leadership is a team sport. There is no such thing as a leader who got anything done alone. It's a myth that a person on a white horse can ride into town and save the people. That belief system has done more harm than any other leadership myth around.

The most trusted source on becoming a better leader

When they wrote their first book, Jim and Barry's approach to writing was more intuitive than trained. Over the years, however, they've noticed a pattern in their writing. They've developed a process that they refer as the Six P's:

1. Point of View
   Each chapter of their book clearly communicates a point of view. Barry and Jim articulate the theme of the section in a sentence or two. It's like a good song. There's one basic message, all the rest is a variation on the theme. They've got reams of data and thousands of stories. Then they summarize all that in a few key messages, the points of view.

2. Practices
   They ask practical questions: What do leaders actually do? What's the behavior that demonstrates the point of view? This part is action-oriented.

3. Principles
   Underlying the points of view and the practices are important guiding principles, learned from years of research. They want their readers to know the principles as well as the prescriptions. To expect people to buy into a message, telling them to do this or do that is not enough. They deserve an explanation about human and organizational behavior without academic jargon.

4. Proof
   What will make a person a more effective leader? What's the evidence that if you do something it will matter? What's the proof that people care about this? Their work is based on solid research and evidence. Their personal credibility is based on that research. Audiences have the right to see proof that what is said works.

5. Parables

   As much as Barry and Jim love research, they understand the power and influence of stories. People are more likely to remember stories than they are to remember numbers. The data provides credibility, but the story teaches. Stories provide examples of the practice and principles in action. Whenever they give a speech or write, they always give an example of a real leader doing real things in order to illustrate the point.

   > In the business world, long-term sustainability is about getting results.

6. Prescriptions

   Their work is prescriptive, not just descriptive. Barry and Jim provide prescriptions in the form of practical action tools. Ultimately, managers and leaders have to go out and put this into practice. In their publisher's research on why people buy business books, the number one thing that the target audience wants is results. They want to be successful – and unless you can help your audience succeed, your probability of establishing a brand is not great. In the business world, long-term sustainability is about getting results. You have to make it practical in order for people to use it. To be responsive to the practical, pragmatic, results-oriented part, they ask themselves, "Would I want to read this book?"

The Six-P method helps Barry and Jim check the quality of their own work, and it differentiates them from the crowd. It's practical, it's credible, and it's easy to understand. They want to communicate in a way that makes people say, "Oh, I see how that works and how I can put it into practice in my own life."

Jim was talking with Ken Blanchard about how Ken's work has endured the test of time. People still buy his *One Minute Manager*, which came out in 1981. Jim asked Ken why their work has had such longevity. Ken said, "When it sticks around for 20 years, I call it the truth." Jim wouldn't be quite that bold, but Ken has a point. When something stands the test of time, it's "tried and true." You can count on it.

> When something stands the test of time, it's "tried and true." You can count on it.

Jim and Barry have stood the test of time because their work is research-based. They feel confident in putting their brand on the cover of a book: "The most trusted source on becoming a better leader." Barry and Jim stand by that statement. It's supported by evidence. It has integrity.

People learn from stories

Not too long ago Jim was in Santa Fe, New Mexico. Santa Fe probably has more fine art galleries per square mile than any other place in the United States, with the exception of New York City. When touring the art galleries, he would stop and ask about the artist, their background and the story behind the painting. Jim has always had this kind of curiosity. He wants to know the story behind everything.

"We all love to hear stories," Jim says. "The sense of being around the collective campfire is exhilarating. It's the reason we read novels and go to movies. We want to be caught up in the experience. It's a universal phenomenon. Story telling is one of the oldest ways in the world to convey values and ideals shared by a community. Before the written word, stories were the means for passing along the important lessons of life. We know how important they are in teaching children, but sometimes we forget how important they are to adults. The intention of stories is not just to entertain. Oh, they're intended to do that for sure, but they're also intended to teach. Good stories move us. They touch us, they teach us, and they cause us to remember. They enable the listener to put the behavior in context and to understand what has to be done in that context in order to live up to expectations."

Jim uses an example from research to illustrate the power of stories. Joanne Martin and Melanie Powers, organizational sociologists from Stanford University, studied the impact of stories on MBA students, a group that is often numbers-driven, highly competitive and skeptical. Martin and Powers compared the impact of four methods of convincing the students that a particular company truly practiced a policy of avoiding layoffs. In one situation, Martin and Powers used only a story to persuade people. In the second, they presented statistical data that showed that the company had significantly lower involuntary turnover than its competitors. In the third, they used the statistics and the story, and in the fourth, they used a straightforward policy statement made by an executive of the company.

We love to hear stories. Good stories move us. They touch us, they teach us, and they cause us to remember.

Which method do you think was most believable to the MBA students? The story-only option was found to be the most believable, followed by story plus data. Statistical data was third, and, as you would expect, the policy statement was the least believable. It makes you wonder why organizations issue a policy statement without presenting an example of how it works in real life. The important point is that stories are not only the most engaging form of communication; they are also the most believable.

Leadership is a personal relationship

In presentations and workshops, Jim often conducts a brief survey with his audience. He lists a number of categories of individuals – teacher, coach, parents, family members, business leader, political leader, entertainer – and asks the audience to indicate from which category (and they get only one) they would say their most important leadership role models come from in their own lives.

Then he shows them the results of a study done with both 18–32 year olds and older adults. The research suggests that people, especially younger people, find role models first and foremost among family members. The next top categories are teachers, coaches and community leaders. In other words, leadership role models don't just come from business. It's about relationships with people who are close to you, relationships that are often formed early in life. Leadership is a relationship; it's personal, and it's emotional. People most distant from us are not role models, despite what the press might report. The people closest to us are much more likely to be those we admire and respect.

> Leadership is a relationship between those who *aspire* to lead and those who *choose* to follow.

As Jim notes, "Leadership is a relationship between those who *aspire* to lead and those who *choose* to follow." Those words – aspire to lead and choose to follow – are carefully selected, because leadership is always an aspiration, never a given. It's in the eye of the beholder. People choose to follow you. They don't follow you if they don't want to. Even if you're in a position of power and influence, people choose whether to put forth more or less energy based on the quality of their relationship with you.

Credibility comes from an emotional connection

If leadership is a relationship, then what is the foundation of leadership? According to Jim and Barry's research, it's *credibility*. "If you don't believe in the messenger, you won't believe the message." What is credible behavior? Credibility is built when you walk the talk, practice what you preach, put

> If you don't believe in the messenger, you won't believe the message.

your money where your mouth is and do what you say you will do. These are the everyday phrases people use to define credibility. Each one of these phrases suggests two things: first, you have to have something to say, and second, you have to back up the words with your actions. That leads to perhaps one of the most unique things that Barry and Jim say: "You cannot do what you say if you have nothing to say. In other words you have to first be clear about what you want to say."

In order to get the highest levels of commitment and achievement, there must be a connection between leaders and their constituents. It goes back to the relationship piece. The first step in the process of becoming a leader is to figure out what you value and what you believe in. The next step is developing a shared vision. That requires a lot of personal reflection, a lot of soul searching, because the evidence tells us that commitment to a cause is driven not by an external force, but by an internal force.

> Brands mobilize people. They get people to take action because there's a connection between them and the message.

To be a believable spokesperson for an organization's vision, it has to resonate with your own vision. You will not be that credible, articulate or passionate as a leader unless you know that the shared vision fits with your core values and believes. As Jim observes, "If I'm going to put a tattoo on my body that tells the world who I am – what I stand for, what symbolically represents me — if I'm going to make a mark, that mark has to be my mark, not someone else's mark. It has to be about me and what's important to me. The flip side is that it has to be important to 'us.' We talk about leaders as mediums between the vision and the people. For example, Martin Luther King talked about freedom. His life was about freedom and justice. He wasn't the first person in the world to talk about freedom and justice. However, he did it in a way that mobilized people. That's what brands do. Brands mobilize people. They get people to take action because there's a connection between them and the message."

Brands lose their appeal once they lose the connection with the customer. Too often, when people talk about personal branding they make the mistake of thinking about "Me, me, wonderful me!" Sure, your clients want to know that you are a credible professional, but they'll be turned off when branding turns into grandstanding. Instead, talk instead about how your brand connects with their values, their needs and their context.

Plenty of brands bring up negative images in people's minds. When brands become so self-centered they begin to lose their edge, you've stopped listening to the customer and stopped hearing the feedback that they're giving you. It's a sure way to kill the brand.

Jim is convinced that a brand needs to be a connection between the idea and the people. People are making a connection with Jim Kouzes and Barry Posner and with their work – an emotional connection. That's critical. The whole concept of branding is that it has to be important to other people. Just putting your smiling face on the cover of your book or promotional material is a meaningless exercise unless it builds an emotional connection. It has to resonate with others. Then people will want to follow, want to buy, and want to use the product or service. Again, credibility is the foundation. All you have to offer is your credibility.

Eight Insights from Jim Kouzes
on Becoming a Leader

1. Leadership is everyone's business. So is personal branding.

2. Leadership isn't about a title or something that you get by somebody appointing you. It's earned through your behavior. It's defined more by the constituents than by you. You only become a leader when other people want to follow you.

3. Be in love with "something." Care deeply about your message. That becomes magnetic, and people are drawn to it.

4. A brand has to be built on substance; it has to be rooted in passion, a meaningful cause or deep commitment. If there is no substance, the brand will not sustain.

5. In the business world, long-term sustainability is about getting results. Give your client results. Give them practical tools that will help them succeed.

6. Be credible. Credibility is built when you walk the talk, practice what you preach, put your money where your mouth is, do what you say you will do. It's the foundation for people to follow you and want to buy your service.

7. Understand your internal force – know what your beliefs are, what your values are, what you aspire to, what excites you, what's important to you, how you do things, the end results of what you want, the means and ends. That requires a lot of personal reflection, a lot of soul searching. Evidence tells us that commitment to a cause is driven not by an external force, but by an internal force.

8. Build an emotional connection between the client and your message. That's what brands do. Brands mobilize people and get people to take action because of that emotional connection.

Jim Kouzes' Viewpoints

On Leadership Practices

Leaders engage in Five Practices of Exemplary Leadership®:

1. *Model the Way*

   Titles are granted, but it's your behavior that wins your respect.

   Leaders must find their own voice, and then they must clearly and distinctively give voice to their values.

   Leaders' deeds are far more important than their words in determining their level of commitment. Words and deeds must be consistent.

2. *Inspire a Shared Vision*

   Leaders cannot commend commitment; they can only inspire it.

   Leaders envision an uplifting and ennobling future.

   Leaders ignite the flame of passion in others by expressing enthusiasm for the compelling vision of their group. Leaders communicate their passion through vivid language and an expressive style.

3. *Challenge the Process*

   Leaders are willing to venture out into the unknown. They search for opportunities to innovate, grow and improve.

   Leaders recognize and support good ideas. They are willing to challenge the system to get new products, processes, services and systems adopted. They take risks and experiment, learning from their inevitable mistakes.

4. *Enable Others to Act*

Leadership is a team effort. Leaders foster collaboration and build trust; they make it possible for others to do good work.

When people are trusted and have more discretion, more authority and more information, they're much more likely to use their energies to produce extraordinary results.

Leaders strengthen others and turn their constituents into leaders themselves.

5. *Encourage the Heart*

Exemplary leaders understand the need to recognize contributions. They focus on clear standards, expect the best, pay attention and personalize recognition.

Exemplary leaders also celebrate the victories of teams, building a sense of community.

On the Future of Leadership

The domain of leaders is the future. The most significant contribution leaders make is not simply today's bottom line; it's the long-term development of people and institutions so they can adapt, change, prosper and grow.

Leadership is hard work, and it's also great fun. Leadership is about caring, about heart and about love.

In the end, leadership development is ultimately self-development. Meeting the leadership challenge is a personal – and a daily – challenge for all of us.[1]

Simon Says:

📖 Read *The Leadership Challenge* by Jim Kouzes and Barry Posner.

The Leadership Challenge, a modern classic on leadership, is about how leaders mobilize others to want to get extraordinary things done in organizations. It's about the practices leaders use to transform values into actions, visions into realities, obstacles into innovations, separateness into solidarity, and risk into rewards. It has been required reading for many students pursuing an MBA, and for good reason. It's practical and the points are very direct, well explained and easy to follow. These ideas have stood the test of time, and are well worth reading and applying.

chapter 11

Three Building Blocks of Personal Brand Management

I have read many books on personal branding, marketing, leadership, personal development and business philosophy. While each book offered insights, not one offered a compelling and proven approach to building a personal brand. Therefore, I decided to develop a model as part of this book. I found that the eight people I profiled have created vibrant and strong brands for themselves because they have done things distinctively in three areas. I call these areas *the three building blocks of personal brand management*:

1. **Essence of You**

   This is the core, the root of who you are. It's your style, background, interests, passion, likes and dislikes, preferred environment, and any other quality that contributes to your identity.

   ➲ Knowing the Essence of You gives you **clarity and authenticity**.

2. Self-Marketing

There are two components of this:

1) Positioning: creating a unique position or perception in other people's minds.

2) Marketing tactics and sales: in some form, you need to get the word out about what you do, who you are and how others can benefit from you. Then you must convince people to spend money on your services.

➲ Effective marketing leads to **visibility and exposure**.

3. Learning

In the process of conducting these interviews, I noticed over and over again how much these thought leaders have invested their time and energy in staying at the cutting edge of their fields. The process of learning includes enhancing knowledge, improving behaviors, building networks and staying mentally and physically fit.

➲ Consistent learning leads to **expertise**.

If you keep focusing and working in those three areas, you will reap the benefits of an electrifying personal brand.

In the end, branding is about authenticity. It's about being real, being you, expressing what's inside, articulating your true values, conveying your beliefs through words, actions and behaviors, and demonstrating what you care about. These things emanate from the heart, which represents your core, your roots, your source. Just as credibility is the foundation for leadership, so is authenticity the source for personal branding.

> "Branding comes from the Gut. From the Heart. In other words: You Gotta Believe! You Gotta Vibrate!"
>
> – Tom Peters, *Re-Imagine*

The Three Building Blocks of Personal Brand Management:

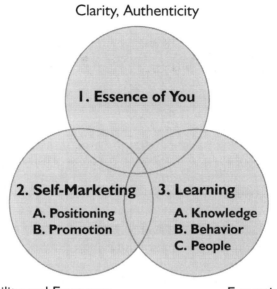

Clarity, Authenticity

1. Essence of You

2. Self-Marketing

A. Positioning
B. Promotion

3. Learning

A. Knowledge
B. Behavior
C. People

Visibility and Exposure   Expertise

1. Essence of You

This is the most important element. From my research and interviews, I learned that without fully understanding a person's essence, it is not possible to create a powerful, sustainable brand.

The Essence of You represents everything about you, the real, authentic you. It's about character, identity, reputation and image – from the way you look to the language you speak; from the things you care most about to the hobbies you enjoy. Specifically, it includes:

- Character, style, appearance, ethnicity
- Your own story, personal history
- Passion, motivation, enthusiasm

- Education, experience, knowledge
- Strengths, abilities, skills, gifts, talents
- Relationships with family, friends, colleagues
- Belief system, self-image, attitude
- Behaviors, habits
- Preferred environments, activities
- Vision, values, ethics

Underlying the Essence of You is the question, "Who am I?" Personally, I found it very hard to answer this question, not only because of the complexity of being human, but because too often, my own ego, ignorance or stubbornness gets in the way. I am still working hard to comprehend my own core, my source, the "authentic Simon." I have spent hundreds of hours in workshops, seminars and classes (as a student and as a teacher). I've read books, completed assessments, and received personal coaching and mentoring to understand myself better. The more I learn about myself, the more I see how much more I can learn. A useful way to understand the roots of your essence is to recap your upbringing and personal history. Here is my abbreviated story:

I grew up in Zollikofen, a town of 8,000 people located a few miles outside of Berne, the capital of Switzerland. I spent eight years there in school and then transferred to a college in Berne – where I graduated with a business Matura (comparable to a Bachelor's degree in the U.S.). After my mandatory year of service in the Swiss Army, I started studying business, economics and marketing at the University of Berne. During my five-year study, I held a variety of jobs: driving a taxi at night in Berne, starting a food-delivery service with friends, working in the marketing department of a major Swiss telecommunications company, doing market research for a consulting company, and giving mountain bike tours in Greece. I learned something from each of those jobs and I enjoyed working with different people and honing new skills. However, I could never say that any of those jobs were my "passion."

At age 26, I moved to Zurich to work as a project manager for an executive seminar provider. I designed, marketed and organized educational programs, conferences and seminars in the areas of strategy, marketing and sales for executives throughout Europe. I loved the job and I had an opportunity to work with and learn from many world-renowned business experts, including Peter Drucker, Gary Hamel, Philip Kotler, Michael Porter, Heinz Dallmer, Heinz Goldmann, Klaus Kleinfeld, Reinhold Rapp, Reinhard Sprenger and many more. It was a blast – but I still didn't get the sense that this was my passion.

I quit my well-paid marketing job in 1997 because I felt the urge to experience life in a country other than Switzerland. I wanted to discover the world and learn about new cultures. So I terminated my apartment lease, packed two suitcases and flew to San Diego to study English at the Center for American English in La Jolla, California. You know the rest of my story from the introduction chapter.

I describe my background for the purpose of illustration. Each of us has our own unique story. From a branding standpoint, it is crucial to delve into the past – to crack our "DNA branding code," as Scott Bedbury puts it in *A New Brand World*. This phrase draws an excellent parallel to the world of biology and chemistry. For the scientist or the research team, it can take a very long time to understand the DNA of a certain species. The odd, sometimes discouraging fact is that when the scientists start with the research, they don't know how long it will take to resolve the issue. It could take months, years or decades. The same is true with people. When we start uncovering our passion, we don't know when it will fully develop. Many people leave this planet without having ever discovered their true purpose. Unfortunately, they die with their music inside them – never having played it.

Knowing your essence means accepting your own life, acknowledging your heritage and the places you lived, accepting your parents and the environment you were raised in, recognizing the people who are close to you, the schools you attended, the jobs you had – these are the foundation of your essence. Since your life is built on this foundation, your brand must include all of these elements of your essence.

Too often, people get caught up in the rat race of making money, striving for the next promotion, comparing themselves with co-workers, buying a bigger house or just keeping up with the endless demands of daily life. Very few take enough time to sit back, contemplate what's important, challenge their assumptions and question their purpose.

"What should I do with my life?" is the question that Po Bronson asked himself. It is also the title of his latest book.[1] He traveled around the country, interviewed hundreds of people from all kinds of backgrounds and wrote up their stories. His book is about people who struggled to unearth their true calling, who dared to be honest with themselves and who faced their own identity. Po learned that many people have all sorts of psychological stumbling blocks, limiting beliefs, misconceptions and deep-rooted fears that prevent them from finding significance and meaning in their lives. Some of those obstacles are:

- The fear that pursuing their passion won't allow them to make enough money.

- The anxiety of not being on a path with a known destination.

- The fear of limiting future options.

- Lack of confidence to appreciate and tell their own story.

- The fear of tearing away from their spouse, family or friends.

- The misconception that life doesn't begin until we find an answer.

Po makes a strong point that we all have passions if we choose to see them. However we have to look inside and backward even more than outside and forward. We have to filter out the chatter that tells us to be someone we are not. We have to liberate ourselves from ideas of what our passion is supposed to be or not supposed to be.

I strongly agree with Po's perspective and I like his suggestion of re-defining success. He writes, "Most people jump through life, asking what's next, and choosing based on where they can make the most money, what offers the most upside or opportunity. A conventional 'success' story is one where, with each *next*, the protagonist has more money, more respect and more possessions. I'd like to suggest an alternative 'success' story – one where, with each *next*, the protagonist is closer to finding that spot where he's no longer held back by his heart and he explodes with talent, and his character blossoms, and the gift he has to offer the world is apparent."[2]

"Well orchestrated brands have depth and richness. They are like personalities, in that the best of them are made interesting and beautiful by a unique blend of interesting and beautiful component parts. It is only in the harmony of the whole that the brand lives."

– Steve Yastrow, *Brand Harmony*

Conclusions about the Essence of You

Interviewing those eight people, interacting with them, studying their work and writing their branding profiles confirmed my previous assumption that people with a strong personal brand have two imperative traits in common:

⮑ **They are authentic.** They know who they are, what they prefer, like, value, care about and are good at. They are clear about the simple yet deep questions: Who am I? Where do I come from? What is unique about me? Why am I here? Fundamentally, they know their purpose in life.

⮑ **They love what they do.** They pursue passion. They are totally committed to their jobs and stand fully behind their work. Their jobs bring joy, fulfillment and personal satisfaction. They are not just working for a paycheck. They live to work. They live intentionally, consciously, on purpose.

2. Self-Marketing

Marketing is about leverage, about spreading your message and letting others know what you do and who you are. You can be the best doctor, the most reliable accountant, the most knowledgeable lawyer or the most sophisticated coach, but if nobody knows about you, you won't get clients. You need to get the word out consistently and often.

A good marketing approach includes two components. First, you position yourself in the client's mind and establish how that client thinks about you. Second, you implement marketing initiatives and focus on sales with the ultimate goal of generating revenue, gaining or retaining a client, or securing a contract.

2A. Positioning Strategies

Positioning is the art of influencing people's perception.

When you project a positive "position" into other people's mind, it helps you stand out in the overcrowded marketplace. You must create a distinguished perception in other people's mind. In other words, build mind share (compared to market share). You accomplish that by being different.[3]

Positioning is not what you do to a service or product; it's what you do to the mind. The better you understand how the mind works, the better you'll understand how positioning works – particularly in an over-communicated society. The following statistics exemplify the rising communication challenge:

- More information has been produced in the last 30 years than in the previous 5,000 years.

- The total of all printed knowledge doubles every four to five years.

- One weekday edition of *The New York Times* contains more information than the average 17th century English person was likely to come across in a lifetime.

- More than 4,000 books are published around the world every day. That is over 1.4 million new books per year!

As a result of the information overload, people are blocking out more and more information as a self-defense mechanism. Jack Trout and Steve Rivkin, in their book *The New Positioning*, list five elements of the mind's selection process:

1. **Minds are limited.**
   Our perceptions are selective. And memory is highly selective.

2. **Minds hate confusion.**
   The best way to enter a mind that hates complexity and confusion is to oversimplify your message. Be smart – keep it simple.

3. **Minds are insecure.**
   Minds tend to be emotional, not rational. When people are uncertain, they often look to others to help

them decide how to act. That's why one of the oldest, most effective devices in advertising is the testimonial.

4. Minds don't change.
In order to change an attitude, it is generally necessary to change a person's beliefs, eliminate old beliefs, or introduce new beliefs.

5. Minds can lose focus.[4]

Capturing other people's attention has become one of the most difficult challenges in today's marketplace. For that reason, it is especially important to simplify your message in order to cut into the mind of your clients. To make a long-lasting impression, you need to be clear and specific about what you offer, who your customer is and why the customer should do business with you.

A positioning strategy will provide that clarity. It is not a marketing slogan. It is meant for internal use as a guideline for your communication. Every aspect of your message should be designed to reinforce your competitive position in the minds of your customers.

Michael Porter, a professor at Harvard Business School and one of the most recognized experts in business strategy and competitive advantage, says that the essence of strategy is that you must set limits on what you're trying to accomplish.[5] Strategy is about making choices and trade-offs. It's about deliberately choosing to be different. Strategy is about the basic value you deliver to customers and which customers you serve. Positioning at that level is where continuity needs to be strongest. Otherwise, it's hard for customers to know what you stand for.

A unique position in other people's mind will give you the leverage to stand out. The foundation of a clear position is a well-defined identity.

"You are in front of the customer only because the customer believes, if only a little bit, that you might be able to better his or her situation."

– Jeffrey Fox, *How to Become a Rainmaker*

2B. Marketing Initiatives and Sales

The second element of self-marketing is reaching out, letting others know of your value proposition and getting in front of decision makers in order to secure a commitment. Ultimately, you want to make a sale, close a deal or get hired.

A sale is the act of landing the deal. To understand sales, it's important to understand why people buy. A recent survey of buyers across the United States asked the question, "Why do you buy where you buy?" The number one reason people buy where they buy is *confidence*, whether it's confidence in the business, in the people, in the product or in the service. The other reasons were, in order, *quality, selection, service* and *price*.

The goal of any marketing initiative is to attract clients, to get the phone to ring or to get a prospective client to walk in the door. There are many different vehicles for marketing – some more effective or expensive than others. The people portrayed in this book chose the tools that matched their style, preference and markets. You'll have to find your own best fit. The magic is in the mix and the consistency. Remember, marketing means that you have something important to say – and you say it well and often.

"The purpose of marketing is to make sales irrelevant."

– Peter Drucker

There is a tremendous amount of material published on marketing, promotion and sales, so I won't get into those details here. Instead I refer to and recommend two books that will give you the knowledge to become a savvy marketer.

1) *How to Become a Rainmaker: The Rules for Getting and Keeping Customers and Clients* by Jeffrey Fox (Hyperion, 2000).

2) *Get Clients Now! A 28-Day Marketing Program for Professionals and Consultants* by C.J. Hayden (American Management Association, 1999).

Conclusions about Self-Marketing

People with a strong personal brand in the professional service field exhibit common characteristics:

➲ **They position themselves effectively in the marketplace.** They have clarity about three questions:
   1. Who is my client? (What is my niche or target market?)
   2. What is my value proposition? (Why should the client buy from me?)
   3. What is unique about me? (What is different about my service or product offering?)

➲ **They are effective marketers.** They have a system in place to extend their message – their expertise – to their market.

The most effective marketing activities are:

• Develop and maintain personal relationships. Follow up; send personal notes or letters; hold in-person meetings; go out for lunch or coffee with someone.

• Network, attend meetings and seminars, serve on committees, collaborate on projects, volunteer.

- Speak at conferences or conventions; give workshops or seminars.
  (Note: all eight people profiled in this book are excellent communicators and speakers. Some use speaking as a major source of income, with five-figure speaking fees).

- Publish. Write books, articles and columns.

- Form alliances or partnerships. Build a referral system.

Some effective tools are:

- Public relations: have stories published about you; get quoted in the media; send press releases.

- Develop a website, send e-newsletters, sell products online.

Less effective tools are:

- Direct mail, brochures and flyers.

- Advertisements in newspaper or magazine classifieds, professional directories, billboards, radio ads.

- Promotional events such as tradeshows and exhibitions.

- Cold prospecting or cold calling.

3. Learning

I am a strong advocate of learning. I am passionate about it. You could call me a learning freak or a learning fanatic. I am glad I am because I believe that learning is imperative, essential – absolutely critical.

In a competitive, global free-agent economy, learning is vital for survival.

The fierce competition in today's global marketplace forces us to be committed to continuous learning, personal renewal and professional development. Learning is about investing in the future of your brand. It's an evolutionary process of expanding your knowledge, mastering skills, gaining new experience, learning an important method. Since learning is an investment – like money – we need to treat it as an investment. Every smart money manager has an investment plan. Talent and brands need a talent/brand development plan.

Being a strong brand demands that you become known for something. This "something" can be:

1) A skill you master and do exceptionally well (e.g. speaking, writing, researching).

2) Specific knowledge or expertise in a certain field (e.g. a real estate agent who knows his neighborhood, its property prices and housing availability better than anyone else).

3) A trait or characteristic you exude (e.g. compassionate, generous, helpful, humorous, a good storyteller).

4) Any combination of the above.

Without exception, all eight people profiled in this book are well known for something specific. Year after year, they have demonstrated a strong commitment to developing themselves as a person and have invested thousands of hours of learning in their lives and careers. They have committed themselves to continuous learning, striving to become the best they can be so that they can set an example and teach others how to do the same.

> Every individual must be committed to a radical program of growth.

I have divided the learning pillar into three components, and each one is equally important. They are:

A. Knowledge
B. Behavior
C. People and networks.

3A. Knowledge

In the information-based economy, the new wealth comes from knowledge. The most valuable assets are no longer tangibles – it's knowledge or intellectual capital. This can be in the form of ideas, reputation, expertise, experience, talent, and access to networks, people or information. The knowledge currency is "social currency on steroids," as Tim Sanders calls it in *Love is the Killer App*.[8] In that book, he promotes the practice of love in business by sharing your intangibles with your business partners: knowledge, network and compassion.

Here are three specific action areas to increase your knowledge assets:

Read

Reading is extremely important, in particular reading books related to your field of interest and expertise. I have been a book-reading enthusiast only for the last five years. In my teen years, I had developed an aversion toward reading. I hated it. Over time, those feelings changed. Reading became easier for me when I chose books that were engaging, entertaining, and connected to my interests. In particular, reading *Losing my Virginity* by Richard Branson was a turning point. His autobiography is fun, enjoyable, uplifting and triggered my appetite for more reading.

> "The person who does not read is no better than the person who cannot read."
>
> – Jeanne Phillips

Now, I go to a bookstore or my local library at least once a month and spend two to three hours there. Each time, I leave with at least three books. The key is to choose valuable books on topics I am passionate about. The biggest challenge is dedicating enough time to read all these books. I set reading as a high priority in my developmental plan because it's a valuable investment with high returns in the future.

I allocate about 80 percent of my reading to business related books and 20 percent to magazines. One of my favorite business magazines is *Fast Company*. It represents a business philosophy that promotes work-life balance, aligns individual values with corporate values, and challenges existing beliefs in the business world.

> "The books you read today will fuel your earning power tomorrow."
>
> – Tim Sanders

Attend learning programs

I use the term learning programs for any event that will enhance your talent. They can range from casual meetings with business associates to multi-day seminars.

I proactively seek out learning programs that will accelerate my learning and talent development. One of them is the Global Institute for Leadership Development (GILD). Organized by Linkage Inc., an international leadership conference provider, GILD is a one-week leadership program that takes place each October in Palm Springs, California. The conference provides a powerful learning platform, a mix of presentations by world-renowned experts, team learning meetings and individual coaching sessions. I am a member of the coaching faculty and work with half a dozen participants during that week, coaching them on specific leadership issues. In addition to my coaching role, I use the event to expand my knowledge and network. It's a very valuable program. You can learn more about it at www.linkage-inc.com.

Another learning component in my career is Toastmasters International. I am a big fan and supporter of this far-reaching organization. It's the undisputed worldwide leader in public speaking training, with over 9,300 clubs and more than 195,000 members in approximately 80 countries. I joined Toastmasters in 1997, the year I came to California, and have been committed ever since then. Our group, about 25 professionals from different backgrounds, meets every Tuesday morning for 75 minutes. We practice public speaking, effective communication, thinking on our feet, giving helpful feedback and much more. I love it because the environment is safe, encouraging and trusting. I have benefited tremendously by increasing my confidence in front of a group, sharpening my presentation skills, building rapport with an audience, persuading others and moving people to take action, just to name a few. I consider Toastmasters one of the most effective and least expensive educational organizations for personal and professional growth. I highly recommend it to anyone who wants to become a more confident communicator.

Listen to audio programs

Every year at our Toastmasters group, we organize a White Elephant fundraising event. It's an auction in which people sell anything to raise money for the club. Many years ago, I purchased a used tape set, *The Psychology of Winning* by Dennis Waitley. I started listening to those six tapes in my car when I drove to client appointments. With no prior experience with audio learning programs, I soon realized what a great use of time it is to learn while driving. Today, many books are available in audio form. By listening to those programs while driving, you can turn your car into a moving university.

3B. Behavior

Behaviors include skills or habits that we have developed over time, intentionally or unintentionally. An intentional skill is usually positive, such as being organized, speaking persuasively to a group, or practicing patience with difficult people. On the other hand, an unintentional habit is often ineffective and hinders performance. Examples include interrupting others, not listening well, procrastination, failure to be punctual and speaking before thinking.

As business professionals, we have to update and upgrade our skill set on a regular basis, just as we do our software programs on our computer. We have to stay sharp and on top of the game.

The foundation of competency and skill is behavior. To improve a skill, we need to change behavior. That's where Marshall Goldsmith' process is relevant. He has applied his method to achieve positive measurable change with thousands of people in various organizations around the world. I use the approach in my own life and career. Last year I set a goal to become more patient, especially to be more calm and confident in stressful situations. I have asked colleagues and friends for feedback – "feedforward" actually – and have gotten valuable ideas and suggestions. One of them is breathing. Many times throughout the day and particularly in demanding situations, I pause, relax and take several deep breaths. As simple as it is, it has been tremendously helpful.

To identify areas to improve, ask yourself the following questions:

- What are the behaviors or skills I need to further develop my talent?

- What are the behaviors that hold me back in achieving my goals?

- If there is one behavior that, if improved over time, would have a significant impact on my effectiveness, balance or happiness, what would that be?

As discussed in Marshall's profile, there are two critical elements to make a lasting, sustainable change in behavior. First, you have to be committed, show a sincere desire and demonstrate ongoing willingness. Second, frequent interaction and follow-up with people around you – family members, friends or colleagues – is a significant factor in making the behavior habitual. This isn't rocket science. If you want to develop a new habit, it takes desire, follow-up and discipline.

John Miller, my friend from A4SL, is also an expert on behavioral change. Recently, he published *Succeed @ Work*, a self-coaching guide and self-study workbook. He suggests a practical six-phase process to make a lasting change in behavior. He suggests engaging a coach or mentor that will guide, support encourage, challenge and keep you on track to achieve your behavioral goal. From my own experience, seeking out and working with a coach or mentor is a powerful way to accelerate learning.

> "A wise man learns more from a fool than ten fools learn from a wise man."
> – Proverb

3C. People and network

In an increasingly complex, interconnected and global world, we depend on others more and more. Creating and maintaining relationships with people through different networks is absolutely crucial. Your rolodex or database – and the emotional connection with those people – is your professional lifeblood. Without it, you will wither away.

Developing solid relationships, staying connected and expanding networks takes time. At the same time, like any well-planned investment, it will give you valuable return. For example, some of the benefits include quick access to information, ideas and knowledge; increased exposure; new opportunities or referrals; and new friends.

> "Our network is proportional to our net worth."
>
> – Tim Sanders

Working with people and developing networks can have many different dimensions. Here are six types of networks that have been most valuable to me:

Alliances and partnerships

For a free agent like myself, belonging to an alliance is the backbone of my business. It's like working for a credible company, but I have full control of my own time. I currently belong to two alliances – Alliance for Strategic Leadership and Marshall Goldsmith Partners – which are related networks with dozens of coaches and consultants. We support each other in marketing and business development, work on client projects together, exchange knowledge, support and refer each other, and sometimes get together socially. Furthermore, I work with other coaches and consultants on a project basis. For example, I work with my friend Mitch Simon, an experienced business coach, to facilitate a 12-session program on generating revenue. It's a fun partnership in which we promote our services and learn from each other.

Professional associations

These are industry-specific groups or special interest organizations. Since most of those are non-profit, they offer valuable volunteer opportunities. Currently, I sit on the board of directors of the San Diego World Trade Center. I learn more about international business while networking with influential people in the San Diego community.

Alumni

The influence of alumni is remarkably strong in the United States, and an often untapped resource. Although I didn't go to school in this country, I do stay in regular contact with my former student colleagues and friends from the University of Berne.

Learning and networking groups

You can form any type of group to foster learning. It can be a referral group, gathering with friends to study a book, discussing a topic of mutual interest, and so on. I consider Toastmasters to be one of my primary learning groups.

Coach, mentor, advisor or trusted friend

These are one-on-one relationships in which you take on the role of the giver or the taker (coach and coachee or mentor and mentee). By teaching others, you gain a better understanding of the subject matter, and enhance your expertise and credibility.

Clients

Working with clients provides various learning opportunities. I have found the most challenging and demanding clients are also the ones teaching me the most valuable lessons.

Take an assessment of the people and networks you associate with. Look at your line of business, its job requirements, your competencies that need strengthening, your level of experience and your personal interests or preferences. Then decide with whom, how, and how often you want to get involved.

New opportunities often show up when we meet new people. When that happens, be prepared. As the saying goes, luck happens when opportunity and preparation meet.

Conclusions about Learning

Learning means growth, renewal and revitalization. It leads to better skills, more knowledge and expertise, and increased talent and brand value. The people profiled in this book have demonstrated a significant commitment towards learning and make it an integral part of their lives, careers and businesses.

➲ **They stay on top of their fields by continuously updating their knowledge, practicing and mastering their skills, and expanding their networks.** They commit to life-long learning to stay fresh and renewed. They are excellent at something because they have invested in themselves.

➲ **They read. They read *a lot*.** Some read one hour a day, others two. They stay on top of things by reading books from experts in their related field.

➲ **They have solid relationships and invaluable connections** – they are highly skilled at networking and building relationships, and spend a lot of time to doing it.

Simon Says:

👪 Join Toastmasters. Go to www.toastmasters.com to find a club in your area. Attend a meeting as a guest and then sign up as a member.

📖 Read *Succeed @ Work: A Workbook for Effective Change*, by John L. Miller. The workbook is available by sending an e-mail to orders@FastBreakPress.com or +1 (805) 492-3400.

✎ Write your own learning/talent development/growth/ renewal plan. Include the following items:

- New skills and competencies (with a plan to acquire them).

- Behaviors to improve (and be emotionally committed).

- Books to read, audio tapes to listen to.

- Knowledge to gain and update.

- People, networks, organizations, coach/mentor, etc.

Review your plan weekly, update it quarterly and discuss it with a trusted colleague or advisor on a regular basis.

Final Word

Competitiveness demands high performance. This is true as much as for business professionals as it is for athletes. Winning an Olympic gold medal, the World Cup, the Super Bowl or the Tour de France requires a winning attitude and the best performance of an entire team.

Winning a new client, getting hired, and getting promoted requires the same. We need to be the best we can be. We need to think and perform like winners. Can we afford not to?

Like the hands of the painter, the voice of the singer and the muscles of the athlete, so is the mind of the business professional. The mind and its skill set are the biggest assets of the business professional. We need to continuously feed the mind, sharpen our thinking and nurture our brain with healthy thoughts.

Beyond all that, all people who perform successfully in any profession have one thing in common: they are fully engaged with their work, enthusiastic and excited about what they do. They show passion, spirit and soul ... all the things that come from within ... the heart of a brand.

Top Ten Rules of Personal Brand Management

Five Insights

1. The experience creates the brand.

2. Personal branding is about how other people perceive you. What really matters is what others believe you can do for them.

3. A genuine personal brand has to be rooted in a meaningful cause, a passion or deep commitment.

4. Strong brands mobilize people. They get people to take action because there's an emotional connection between the brand, the message and the client.

5. Brand recognition builds when people who have never met you know who you are.

Five Commandments

1. Identify and recognize the Essence of You. That becomes your uniqueness and distinguishing factor.

2. You have to love what you are doing. Do what you are passionate about; what you care about; what excites you; what gets you up in the morning.

3. Always know who your customers are and what they want. Really understand the clients' issues, challenges and problems; then provide a solution.

4. Find something you can do better than anybody else. Then become really, really good at that.

5. Create visibility and get exposure; speak, write, network, do public relations, or anything else that gets your name out.

   Bonus: Find a topic that is not yet covered, and become an expert on that topic.

Suggested Reading

As you strive to develop and manage your own personal brand, I highly recommend the following books:

Personal and Career Development

1. **What Should I Do with My Life?** by Po Bronson (Random House, 2002).

   In an authentic, engaging and vivid voice, Bronson profiles 50 business professionals who have gone through major job transitions in search of their true calling. A fun, inspiring and thought provoking read.

2. **Whistle While You Work: Heeding Your Life's Calling**, by Richard J. Leider and David A. Shapiro (Berrett-Koehler Publishers, 2001).

   Everyone has a calling, "the inner urge to give your gifts," as the authors define it. Their book is a practical blueprint for making a living doing what you were born to do. It shows a way to deliberately choose a way of life and work consistent with your uniqueness.

3. **The Psychology of Winning: Ten Qualities of a Total Winner**, by Dr. Denis Waitley (Berkley Publishing Group, 1992). Also available on audiotape.

   Being a winner is a way of thinking, based on attitude and self-concept. Waitley offers simple yet profound principles of healthy thought and behavior that give you the winning edge in every situation. His book is one of my favorites in the area of developing human potential.

4. **Think and Grow Rich**, by Napoleon Hill (Ballantine Books, reissued 1987).

   This is an inspirational classic. Written over 60 years ago, Hill provides well-researched, universal principles for life. With definiteness of purpose, persistence, and a burning desire, you can translate thoughts into things.

5. **How to Be a Great Communicator – In Person, on Paper and on the Podium**, by Nido R. Qubein (Wiley, 1996).

    Your power to influence the lives of others is as great as your ability to communicate. This book offers a wealth of insights on communicating with diverse audiences in an engaging and powerful way.

6. **The Platinum Rule: Discover the Four Basic Business Personalities and How They Can Lead You to Success**, by Tony Alessandra and Michael J. O'Connor (Warner Books, 1998).

    Alessandra offers a unique concept and the tools to determine personality types, as well as guidelines on interacting in the most effective way with each type.

8. **Love It, Don't Leave It – 26 Ways to Get What You Want at Work**, by Beverly Kaye and Sharon Jordan-Evans (Berrett-Koehler Publishers, 2003).

    This book will teach you to find satisfaction in your work – right now, without waiting for the perfect circumstances.

7. **The Leader of the Future: New Visions, Strategies and Practices for the Next Era**, by Marshall Goldsmith and Richard Beckhard (Jossey-Bass, 1997).

    Over 30 essays on cutting-edge business leaders, each offering a unique perspective on the direction of leadership in the future.

8. **Ready for Anything: 52 Productivity Principles for Work and Life**, by David Allen (Viking Books, 2003).

    Universal principles for mastering the balance of work and life. A practical resource for anyone looking to create a stress-free, productive life.

9. **The Leadership Challenge** (Third Edition), by Jim Kouzes and Barry Posner (Jossey-Bass, 2003).

    A modern classic on leadership, this book offers

essential perspectives on mobilizing others to achieve at an extraordinary level. With insights on transforming values into practices, obstacles into victories, and risk into rewards, it is both practical and visionary.

10. **Succeed @ Work**, by John L. Miller (Fast Break Press, 2004). A self-coaching workbook designed to help readers become more effective at work. The book helps readers identify what to change and how to successfully adopt more satisfying and effective behaviors.

Branding, Marketing and Sales

11. **A New Brand World: 8 Principles for Achieving Brand Leadership in the 21st Century**, by Scott Bedbury with Steven Fenichell (Penguin Books, 2001).
    Bedbury's approach to branding is genuine and reasonable. I enjoyed his own stories of branding from his experience at Nike and Starbucks. A book I recommend to any marketer.

12. **How to Become a Rainmaker: The Rules for Getting and Keeping Customers and Clients**, by Jeffrey J. Fox (Hyperion, 2000).
    Fox offers practical, common sense advice to grow revenue. A short, sweet book about basic key success factors in sales. His ideas have increased my own sales.

13. **Get Clients Now! A 28-Day Marketing Program for Professionals and Consultants**, by C.J. Hayden (American Management Association, 1999).
    I recommend this book to professional service providers who need a more systematic approach to marketing. It provides a simple framework and realistic tips to attract more clients.

Business Philosophy and Trends

14. **Love is the Killer App: How to Win Business and Influence Friends**, by Tim Sanders (Three Rivers Press, 2002).

    Sanders introduces a different way of thinking into the business world. I believe his philosophy is the future. An absolute must read!

15. **Re-imagine!** by Tom Peters (Dorling Kindersley Publishing, 2003).

    In a bold, provocative format, Peters challenges existing business practices and offers innovative ideas to deal with the chaotic and unpredictable business reality. Even though I don't agree with everything Peters writes, we need to take his viewpoints very seriously.

16. **Free Agent Nation: How America's New Independent Workers are Transforming the Way We Live**, by Daniel H. Pink (Warner Business Books, 2001).

    Free Agent Nation presents the reasons why more and more people choose to be free agents: they aspire to more satisfaction, security and significance. If you do – or want to – work for yourself, this book is for you.

References

Chapter 1: The New Business Landscape

1. Beth Belton. "Tech Advances Raise Job Insecurity." *USA Today* (February 17, 1999).

2. Jennifer Reingold. "Into Thin Air." *Fast Company* (April 2004).

3. Tom Peters, *Re-imagine!* (Dorling Kindersley Publishing, 2003) page 55.

4. Daniel H. Pink, *Free Agent Nation: How America's New Independent Workers are Transforming the Way We Live* (Warner Business Books, 2001) page 35.

5. Pink, *Free Agent Nation*, page 19.

6. Pink, *Free Agent Nation*, page 14.

7. Abraham H. Maslow. "A Theory of Human Motivation." *Psychological Review*, Volume 50, 1943 (Harper and Bros, 1954) pages 370 – 396.

8. Pink, *Free Agent Nation*, page 78.

9. Pink, *Free Agent Nation*, page 79.

10. "War for Talent II: Seven Ways to Win", *Fast Company* (January 2001) page 98.

Chapter 2: Personal Branding Philosophy

1. Scott Bedbury with Steven Fenichell, *A New Brand World: 8 Principles for Achieving Brand Leadership in the 21st Century* (Penguin Books, 2001).

2. Tim Sanders, *Love Is the Killer App: How to Win Business and Influence Friends* (Three Rivers Press, 2002) page 36.

Chapter 3: Nido Qubein – Being Focused

Nido Qubein's profile is based on an interview with the author on September 12, 2003.

1. Nido Qubein's Viewpoints are from "Ten Principles of Motivation." *The Toastmaster* (February 2004) pages 14-15.

Chapter 4: Tony Alessandra – Finding Your Voice

Tony Alessandra's profile is based on an interview with the author on August 28, 2003.

1. Extracted from "About the Platinum Rule," an article posted on Tony Alessandra's website (http://www.alessandra.com/about_platinumrule/about_platinum.asp).

2. Tony Alessandra's Viewpoints are extracted from several articles on his website (www.allesandra.com) and his e-zine, "Dr. T's Timely Tips."

Chapter 5: Beverly Kaye – Discover Your Niche

Beverly Kaye's profile is based on an interview with the author on August 13, 2003.

1. Marshall Goldsmith, Beverly Kaye and Ken Shelton. *Learning Journeys* (Davies-Black Pub, 2000) pages 155 –158.

2. Beverly Kaye's Viewpoints are extracted from *Love It, Don't Leave It – 26 Ways to Get What You Want at Work* by Beverly Kaye and Sharon Jordan-Evans (Berrett-Koehler Publishers, 2003).

Chapter 6: Marshall Goldsmith – Becoming Well Known

Marshall Goldsmith's profile is based on an interview with the author on March 14, 2003.

1. Marshall Goldsmith and Howard Morgan. "Leadership is a Contact Sport." *strategy+business* (September 2004). This

article contains research involving over 86,000 respondents. It documents the impact of ongoing interaction in increasing leadership effectiveness.

2. Marshall Goldsmith's Viewpoints are extracted from his website (www.marshallgoldsmith.com) and several of his published articles.

Chapter 7: David Allen – Increasing Personal Productivity

David Allen's profile is based on an interview with the author on October 13, 2003.

1. David Allen's Viewpoints are extracted from *Ready for Anything: 52 Productivity Principles for Work and Life* by David Allen (Viking Books, 2003).

Chapter 8: Gayle Carson – Making Things Happen

Gayle Carson's profile is based on an interview with the author on March 5, 2004.

1. Gayle Carson's Viewpoints are extracted from her e-zine, *Wiz of Biz Tip* (www.gaylecarson.com).

Chapter 9: Brian Tracy – Pushing to the Front

Brian Tracy's profile is based on an interview with the author on June 8, 2003.

1. Brian Tracy, *Success is a Journey: Make Your Life a Grand Adventure* (Excellence Publishing, 1998).

2. Brian Tracy's Viewpoints are extracted from his books and website (www.briantracy.com).

Chapter 10: Jim Kouzes – Becoming a Leader

Jim Kouzes' profile is based on an interview with the author on November 17, 2003.

1. Jim Kouzes' Viewpoints are extracted from his book *The Leadership Challenge* (Jossey-Bass, 2003).

Chapter 11: Three Building Blocks of Personal Brand Management

1. Po Bronson, *What Should I Do with My Life?* (Random House Trade Paperbacks, 2003).

2. Bronson, *What Should I Do with My Life?* page 222.

3. Al Ries and Jack Trout, *Positioning – The Battle for Your Mind* (McGraw-Hill, 2000).

4. Jack Trout and Steve Rivkin, *The New Positioning – The Latest on the World's #1 Business Strategy* (McGraw-Hill, 1997).

5. Michael Porter, professor at the Harvard Business School, adviser to U.S. and foreign governments, and author of the best-selling book *Competitive Strategy: Techniques for Analyzing Industries and Competitors* (Free Press, 1998).

6. Murray Raphel, *Up the Loyalty Ladder: Turning Sometime Customers into Full-Time Advocates of Your Business* (Harpercollins, 1995).

7. Sanders, *Love Is the Killer App*, page 67.

8. Sanders, *Love Is the Killer App*.

About the Author

Simon Vetter advises and coaches business professionals in personal brand management, behavioral change and leadership development. He is an executive coach and consultant for the Alliance for Strategic Leadership (A4SL).

Simon has 17 years experience in marketing, sales and leadership development. Prior to joining A4SL, he was a salesman, trainer, and consultant for a multinational training organization. He taught programs in communication, leadership, presentation, customer service and teambuilding. Prior to his 1997 relocation to San Diego, he designed and marketed executive programs and management seminars in Europe.

Over the course of his career, he has worked with executives and coached leaders from 3M, ABB, Berlex Laboratories, Bertelsmann, CalPERS, Diversa, Lufthansa, IBM, J. Walter Thompson, Johnson & Johnson, Neal Electric, Procter & Gamble, RE/MAX International, San Diego World Trade Center, Siemens and others.

Simon earned the equivalent of the Master's degree in Business and Marketing from the University of Berne, Switzerland, and is fluent in English, German and French. He grew up in Switzerland and now lives in San Diego, California.

For more information, visit Simon's website: www.simonvetter.com.

For Additional Copies of This Book

Online orders: www.simonvetter.com

E-mail orders: orders@simonvetter.com

Telephone orders: +1 (858) 793-6279

Postal orders: 910 Stratford Court, Del Mar, CA 92014 USA

Please send me *STAND OUT! Branding Strategies for Business Professionals*

Qty. _____ $17.95

Sales Tax: Please add 7.25% for all orders shipped to California addresses ($1.31 per book).

Shipping: For orders to be shipped to U.S. addresses, please add $4.00 for the first book and $2.00 for each additional book. For international orders, add $9.00 for the first book and $5.00 for each additional book.

Please send me more FREE information on:

☐   Upcoming speaking engagements

☐   Branding seminars/courses

☐   Consulting and coaching services

Name: _____

Street Address: _____

City: _____ State: _____ Zip: _____

Country: _____

Telephone: _____

E-mail address: _____

Personal checks and money orders accepted. No credit cards accepted at this time.

For Additional Copies of This Book

Online orders: www.simonvetter.com

E-mail orders: orders@simonvetter.com

Telephone orders: +1 (858) 793-6279

Postal orders: 910 Stratford Court, Del Mar, CA 92014 USA

Please send me *STAND OUT! Branding Strategies for Business Professionals*

Qty. _____ $17.95

Sales Tax: Please add 7.25% for all orders shipped to California addresses ($1.31 per book).

Shipping: For orders to be shipped to U.S. addresses, please add $4.00 for the first book and $2.00 for each additional book. For international orders, add $9.00 for the first book and $5.00 for each additional book.

Please send me more FREE information on:

☐ Upcoming speaking engagements

☐ Branding seminars/courses

☐ Consulting and coaching services

Name: _____

Street Address: _____

City: _____ State: _____ Zip: _____

Country: _____

Telephone: _____

E-mail address: _____

Personal checks and money orders accepted. No credit cards accepted at this time.

RIT - WALLACE LIBRARY
CIRCULATING LIBRARY BOOKS

OVERDUE FINES AND FEES FOR <u>ALL</u> BORROWERS

- Recalled = $1/ day overdue (no grace period)
- Billed = $10.00/ item when returned 4 or more weeks overdue
- Lost Items = replacement cost+$10 fee
- All materials must be returned or renewed by the duedate.